For Nancy and Bill

as you journey towards Bethlehem

may these words light your way

Sean

11/19/17

Destination Bethlehem

ALSO BY J. BARRIE SHEPHERD

Between Mirage and Miracle: Selected Poems for Seasons, Festivals, and the Occasional Revelation

Faces by the Wayside: Persons Who Encountered Jesus on the Road

Whatever Happened To Delight? Preaching the Gospel in Poetry and Parables

Aspects of Love: An Exploration of 1 Corinthians 13

Faces at the Cross: A Lent and Easter Collection of Poetry and Prose

Faces at the Manger: An Advent-Christmas Sampler of Poems, Prayers, and Meditations

Seeing With the Soul: Daily Meditations on the Parables of Jesus in Luke

The Moveable Feast: Selected Poems for the Christian Year and Beyond

A Pilgrim's Way: Meditations for Lent and Easter

A Child Is Born: Meditations for Advent and Christmas

Praying the Psalms: Daily Meditations on Cherished Psalms

Prayers from the Mount: Daily Meditations on the Sermon on the Mount

Encounters: Poetic Meditations on the Old Testament

A Diary of Prayer: Daily Meditations on the Parables of Jesus

Diary of Daily Prayer

Destination Bethlehem

Daily Meditations, Prayers, and Poems
to Light the Way to the Manger

J. Barrie Shepherd

WIPF & STOCK · Eugene, Oregon

DESTINATION BETHLEHEM
Daily Meditations, Prayers, and Poems to Light the Way to the Manger

Wipf & Stock
An Imprint of Wipf and Stock Publishers
199 W. 8th Ave., Suite 3
Eugene, OR 97401

www.wipfandstock.com

ISBN 13: 978-1-4982-0922-9

Manufactured in the U.S.A.

I dedicate this book to our neighbors and fellow residents,
the staff, and the administration
of Piper Shores Retirement Community,
perched on the rocky Atlantic coast of Scarborough, Maine,
with thanks to God
that they found "room at the inn"
for Mhairi, Iona, and me.

Let us now go even unto Bethlehem,
and see this thing which is come to pass,
which the Lord hath made known unto us.

—LUKE 2:15 (KJV)

Contents

PERMISSIONS

Permission to reprint the following poems has been granted.

From *The Christian Century*:
Advent Awakening, Repetition, Early Advent, Christmas Mail, Advent Haiku, Advent Saturday Morning, Trimming, Lighting the Advent Candles, The Messiah, Incarnating, The Morning After, Essence, On the 11th Day of Christmas, Hanging the Greens, The Coming of the Light

From *Presbyterian Outlook*:
Advent Invitation, Advent Opening Bell, Early Advent, Time to be Careful, Advent Candles, Advent's Secret, Seasonal Décor, Nothing for Christmas, Minimizing Magic, December Eighteenth, Pre-Nativity, Don't Stop Me, Nativity, On the 11th Day of Christmas

From *Weavings*:
Advent Awakening, Kaleidoscoping Christmas, The Silent Seers, The Midwife of Bethlehem

From *The Living Church*:
Advent's Secret, Stall for Christmas, Late Call, Wish

From *The Swarthmorean*:
Trimming, The Morning After

Permissions

From *Christianity Today:*
Advent Candles

From *Theology Today:*
Left Behind

From *The Cresset:*
Herod's Dream

PREFACE

Christmas has always seemed the busiest of times; and for someone with the double-barreled name and job title I bear—Pastor Shepherd—it can seem even more so. All the normal Yuletide pressures and deadlines are topped by the one that looms at midnight or, to be more accurate, eleven p.m. on December twenty-fourth: the annual Christmas Eve sermon. And the more years spent facing this challenge, the more daunting it becomes. All the best lines have already been exhausted by the Christmas carols, and your own dwindling supply gets more and more picked over until it starts to look like the bargain basement after the January sales . . . a sock here . . . a glove there . . . and very little worth checking out at all.

Yet another annual complication was the cherished tradition, in one college town where I served for sixteen such Christmas Eves, of having a live Santa (played by a band of high school and college lads) visit your children in their bedrooms and present them with merry "Ho Ho Hos," plus a previously selected small gift. The youngsters loved it. But, since I was never home from the midnight service before one-thirty a.m., the Shepherd household needed to be placed at the end of the list. Consequently, those—by then not quite so merry—"Ho Ho Hos" seldom sounded at our front door before three in the morning. Only after that could "Mama in her kerchief and I in my cap" finally "settle down for an (extremely brief) winter's nap."

Nowadays, with no midnight sermons to deliver, and no one left at home to wait up for Santa, I get to bed much earlier on Christmas Eve, but find myself missing some of the excitement and challenge of those earlier days. Considering all this, I realized that it has been almost twenty-five years since the publication of my *Faces at the Manger*, a few years longer since *A Child is Born* first appeared; and while these two slim volumes still seem to bear a significant message for the new reader, those who have already found them helpful across the years might appreciate the opportunity to look at something fresh and somewhat different. So I decided to look back at some of those well-worn traditions, to check over some of those carefully crafted sermons, to see if anything there might be salvaged, or better say, reclaimed, even recycled. In the thrifty spirit of my Scottish homeland, and new ideas and perspectives being scarce in any of our seasons, I began to sift through the homiletical mementos of those long and weary "nights before Christmas," looking for tales to be retold, gems to be repolished, gifts to be reopened.

It is my hope and prayer that, recaptured here and set within a holiday wreath of poetry and prayer, these Advent/Christmas meditations might open up a way for you, dear reader, to pause a moment in these hectic days, to reflect, perhaps, on some of your own cherished Christmases past, to find yourself a welcoming spot beneath the tree, a quiet place beside the manger.

I have arranged these selections to follow the traditional sequence of Advent, providing a meditation, prayer, and/or poetry, for each day of the season's four weeks. In addition there is a series of meditations and poems for Christmas Eve and Christmas Day, and a final selection covering the period between Christmas and Epiphany, including New Year. A few of the poems are specifically dated. I ask the reader's indulgence when such dates do not correspond with the actual days of the Advent calendar in any particular year.

As I look back, in putting this book to rest, over some four-score Christmas celebrations of my own, I feel profoundly thankful for all that this warmest and most welcoming season has added to those years, and pray that my words may call forth a similar grateful response from all who read them.

Piper Shores, Scarborough, Maine
Epiphany 2015

ACKNOWLEDGMENTS

A debt of gratitude is owed to the faithful readers, colleagues, and friends who have supported and encouraged me in the writing of this, my sixteenth book. Particular thanks to Mhairi, my wife of fifty-one years, for her careful reading of this text, her editorial skills, fact checking, grammatical expertise, and her gently remedial observations whenever the preacher within me attempted to prevail.

Last Sunday in November

THE MANGER CALLS AGAIN

and for all the humdrum daily-ness
of places, things, and persons too,
all the sheer predictability
of politics and power—those same-old,
same-old headlines on the news—
for all the dwindling of these days
so that the memory far outweighs
the flimsy realm of possibility and promise,
still one rummages for candle-stubs and matches,
turns thoughts toward new ways to bring delight,
a fleeting sense, at least, of generosity both given
and received, then folds the hands in prayer
that this season's secret music might—
before it's vanished in thin air—
lift all our lives in momentary,
yet still mending melody.

HOMELAND SECURITY

(Eve of Advent)

Times like these—
what with daily news of terror,
the random ways of cold malevolence,
fanatic dedication to the cause of savage death—
the customary comforts of this season
can seem thin, at best,
and threadbare,
offering scant protection
from December's chill and dying days.

Times like these
may yet recall a child
whose birth was also framed
by bloodshed, and a bleak indifference,
who found seeming scant protection
in a mother's arms, a father's watchful wisdom,
that old, eternal tenderness, whose shield
is nevertheless the only, sure, and best defense
against the savage dark.

AT THE BRINK

There is a mild portending in the air
this last November morning,
a persistent wish
that, with tomorrow's wreath
and purple candles, at least something will begin,
or should I say, "begin again."
Almost eighty of these now, after all,
and still—like weary Simeon—
I'm scanning faces for him, seeking, hoping,
perhaps fearing.

If he did come in the end, how would I know him?
Would there be certain words exchanged,
a knowing look, even a fierce embrace?
Might I have already missed whatever is to come,
failing to recognize the fathoms, deep beneath the daily pageant?
Or will this be the year when ancient word and melody,
rich color, and the candled scent of evergreen,
bear light to life and everlasting joy
within these timeworn, aching bones?

Advent Week One

Sunday

SOMETHING FOR CHRISTMAS I
Something Worth Hoping For

*. . . we rejoice in our hope of sharing the glory of God. More than that
we rejoice in our sufferings, knowing that suffering produces endurance, and endurance produces character, and character produces
hope, and hope does not disappoint us.*

—ROMANS 5:2–3

If ever there was a season set aside for hoping, surely this is it.
From the gleam in the eyes of little children as they survey the
glittering cornucopia spread before them in stores, catalogs, and
computers, to the blinking lights in the windows, and on the cal-
culators of the merchants, there does seem to be a whole lot of
hoping going around in these pre-Christmas days.

And, to be completely fair, it is not all selfish, acquisitive, or
materialistic hoping that we see. There is something about this
season—be it the music, the lights and decorations, the messages
and packages, fond memories evoked—that can bring out in even
the most worn-down and worn-out of us the hope for better times,
for a more trusting, welcoming way of life. For so many of us these
weeks before Christmas become all wrapped up with hope.

It is only when we stop to ask, "but what kind of hope is this,
just what manner of hoping are we dealing with here?" that questions, significant questions, begin to arise. This word "hope" finds
its origins, so the scholars suggest, in an Anglo-Saxon root, a root
that signifies "the opening of the eyes." But far too much of what is
called "hope" nowadays seems to be based on the opposite of this,

not the opening, but the deliberate closing of the eyes. "Hope is a tease," as the Dowager Marchioness of Grantham—Maggie Smith's character—remarks on *Downton Abbey*, " . . . a tease to prevent us from accepting reality."

It seems true to say that the only way many of us can even *hope* to hope today is by closing our eyes tight against a sad series of harsh realities—realities of a cruel world one cannot help but glimpse, right before the Christmas TV specials, on the nightly news. Hope, for many folk, in other words, is a rosy-colored-spectacles experience, a therapeutic luxury, to be indulged in only upon certain limited occasions. While in the background, in to-day's culture—which is not so much a *Culture of Disbelief,* as one recent writer described it, as it is a Culture of Disappointment, of Disillusionment—there lingers that twenty-first century, sophisticated cynicism, the realization that, as some wag once put it, "The lion may well lie down with the lamb, but that lamb is not going to get much sleep." Or as Archy, resident cockroach at the *New York Sun*, typed to his editor, Don Marquis the poet:

> the only way boss
> to keep hope in the world
> is to keep changing its
> population frequently

Persian poet, Omar Khayyam, expressed all of this, in elegant phrases, for an earlier generation:

> The Worldly Hope men set their hearts upon
> Turns Ashes—or it prospers; and anon,
> Like Snow upon the Desert's dusty Face
> Lighting a little hour or two—is gone.[1]

I was tempted to title this meditation, "A Shocking Hope," be-cause, in studying the Scriptures on this theme—and these Scrip-tures (particularly the New Testament) are filled with references to hope—I discover a vastly different picture. There is, in fact, very little of what today one might call "optimism" in the Bible, if there

---

1. Khayyam, *Rubaiyat.*

is any at all. The people who shaped these holy books, who compiled these ancient, living manuscripts within the context of their own lives, their daily wrestling with faith and fear, were not in any position to indulge in that kind of hoping. They usually had very little going for them, practically nothing really to build hope upon. They were among the earliest of Christians, the very fact of whose faith meant that they were living in the constant shadow of public denunciation, imprisonment, trial, and terrifying death. There was no way, no matter how they might have wanted to, to close their eyes to these grim realities that stared them in the face. They were just too close for that kind of comfort.

And so one finds here a different, an alternative kind of hope. Look again at how Paul described it in Romans:

> . . . we rejoice in our hope of sharing the glory of God. More than that we rejoice in our sufferings, knowing that suffering produces endurance, and endurance produces character, and character produces hope, and hope does not disappoint us because God's love has been poured into our hearts.

"Suffering . . . endurance . . . character . . . hope." That's the route hope followed for Paul, that's the family tree of this New Testament type of hoping: from suffering, through endurance, into character, and then, finally, achieving hope. This is a hope which, far from shutting its eyes, far from ignoring or fleeing from suffering, springs directly from the heart of anguish and pain; a hope which, far from any passing mood or momentary sentiment, any blind and easy optimism, is born within the soul that has endured, and in endurance has gained that—so rare—attribute of these times, character. And *character* produces hope.

On a wall in the darkest, deepest crypt of Germany's Cologne Cathedral there are words traced by a trembling, yet still hopeful hand. Seven Jews lay hidden there during the darkest days of World War II, seven children of Father Abraham, their pitiful bundles of possessions gathered round them, concealed through the courage and faith of the Archbishop of Cologne. And sometime in the night, those darkest hours of human desolation and despair, one of them reached out and scratched upon that wall these words, not of optimism—that would be absurd, if not obscene in such circumstances—these words of genuine and authentic hope:

I believe in the dawn, even though it be dark.
I believe in God, even though He be silent.

This hope that arises from suffering, this miraculous hope born in the deepest of darkness . . . a shocking hope indeed among these merry marketing days of "Ho, Ho, Ho!" and holiday cheer. A bit of a downer, to be completely honest, this must seem for many today, considering the sought-after spirit of this season. But a hope, nevertheless, that folk can see, actually see with their eyes wide open, and therefore a hope that might last beyond the unwrapping of the last Christmas package, the popping of the final New Year cork. Paul described it as the hope that does not—as so many of these present passing hopes will do—disappoint us.

What is it like then, this shocking hope, this biblical hope, this hope that grows from suffering, through endurance, to character, and then blossoms into full-fledged bloom? The Hebrew word for hope has the root meaning of "to twist or twine" and is related to the word *kivin*, the word for a spiderweb. So much of our hoping has this spiderweb quality to it, this quality of surprising strength out of seeming weakness, of stunning beauty woven from the tiny, apparently insignificant strands of daily living. We live in, we live by, an interwoven network of hopes, each one lending strength to the others, and all of them, however fragile, somehow supporting us, leading us into the future.

I tramped the hills above my Scottish hometown several years ago. It was a chill but bright November morning with the northern sun barely rising above the trees. My mother was desperately ill, dying, as I had suspected was the case. But she was to come to church that Sunday, and I, home from America on a farewell visit, was to be the preacher. I was grappling for the words, words to preach the Gospel in a way that would speak to her, and to all who heard, about this gift, this experience, we Christians call hope. And then I saw it, glimpsed and knew the glory all about me. The grassy pasture field on my right hand was caught and held, illuminated at a curious angle, by that low-on-the-horizon winter sun. A breeze, chill but somehow playful, blew across the close-cropped surface of the turf. And there I glimpsed an astonishing spectacle, a shining, silken, network of microscopically thin spiderwebs all linking blade-to-blade-to-blade of grass. There must have been thousands upon thousands of them, forming a shimmering, gossamer blanket all across that ordinary/heavenly meadow, and moving, lifting, waving lightly in the wind. I sat beside the hedgerow spellbound. I'd never seen such a thing, never even guessed such things existed. And as I sat and watched I found a healing, and a hope renewed, a magic, in the best and holiest sense of that word, a firm and steady reassurance that glory—yes, *the glory of the Lord*—shall be revealed. And that our hope is not, will not ever be in vain.

It cannot be all that defined, this fragile, formidable, spiderweb we claim and cling to. If it could it would not be hope, but plan or goal, reward even; and true hope is not like that. It is an experience; and experience can never be fully described. It is a reality, not just a projection; and no one has yet come close to pinning down, explaining reality. Like those mysterious, bulky packages that appear and disappear around the home during this season, hope has to be unknown, or it wouldn't be hope at all.

Yet there are a few things we *can* say about this hope, this hope we are given to get by with. It has something to do with birth—this much is sure—but with an unexpected, seemingly quite inappropriate birth, one that no one will believe is really true, the right one, in the right place, at the right time, under the proper circumstances.

It has something to do with peace—this too seems certain. But, once again, not the kind of peace that we desire, or think we hope for. It will be a peace that will surprise us, shock us, drive us to our knees, a peace that will demand nothing, nothing of us except our entire selves.

It has something to do with mystery—this cannot be doubted—prophecies, kings, and seers, astrologers and virgins, stars, shepherds, sheep, and angels. And this mystery, too, is hard to recognize, even to look for, in this eminently practical, common-sense, dollars-and-cents, all too literally down-to-earth world. It will boggle the mind when it comes, our hope, shock our rationalistic heads all the way through into eternity.

It has something to do with a baby—we know this much also—and so we should be especially attentive in these latter days to children, seeing in them a sign, a promise, a foretaste of this hope we are allowed to share without ever really grasping it.

It has everything to do with God—of this we can be certain—the power that gives us life and takes life from us, the source of all the gifts with which we bless and curse ourselves along the way. Hope has everything to do with God, and with trusting ourselves to God, and with recognizing, all around us, the life God pours out for us this and every day, until our hope is no longer hope, because it has become Immanuel—God with us.

A shocking hope. A hope born in the midst of suffering. A hope that finds its home within that fragile, yet enduring web of mystery and promise. Not much to hope for, to hang on to there, is there? Yet, think about it for a moment. Is this not the only kind of hope that can *be* hope in a world like this one, a world which cost the Son of God his life, still costs the lives of forty-thousand children who die of hunger each and every day? If it won't play in a cancer ward, as a wise man once taught me, then whatever it is it is not the gospel. And neither is it hope, the hope we have in Christ. Keeping your eyes open . . . That's what that Anglo-Saxon root implies, and what Mark's gospel tells us:

> Watch therefore—for you do not know when the master
> of the house will come . . . And what I say to you I say to
> all: "Watch." (Mark 13:35–37).

To be in hope this time of year is to keep our eyes open, open for each and every moment when the light shines in the darkness, when the mystery at the heart of it all reveals itself, unveils itself. But that means looking deep into the dark, not gazing at the tree lights till it all becomes a multicolored blur. That means finding, in the hospitals and homeless shelters, the lonely hearts and empty hands about us, and within us, the meaning of it all, the secret, not just of this festival of light, but of the feast of life itself, that truth beyond all death, that life, true life is born, begins, and never ever ends, in love.

∼

Now may the God of hope fill us with all joy and peace in believing, so that, by the power of the Holy Spirit, we may abound in hope. Amen.

Monday

A Prayer to Open Advent

For a gray November sky
with a filigree of bare branches
outlined against one patch of blue,
for random swatches of bright gold and scarlet
fallen around the bases of tall trees,
for the calling of the geese on the move overhead,
their trailing, V-shaped skeins lifting eyes and hearts
to the heavens and beyond,
for a touch of frost on the lawn,
and that feathery first flake of falling snow,
for family tables circled with fond laughter, honest prayer,
bright candles, good food, rich stories, new and old,
the young ones, the not-so-young,
the cheery, noisy moments, the quiet, thoughtful ones,
for long and easy walks with dogs,
crackling log fires, bright colored cards in the mail,
remembrances of folk and moments almost now forgot,
yet still bearing a light and lingering joy,
so many gifts, so many blessings
to thank you for, our God,
in this past week of high Thanksgiving.

And now we turn again toward the manger.
We begin to trace once more those familiar,
age-old hopes and dreams, prophecies in song and story,
well-worn traditions of both church and fireside.
We make plans for moments of rejoicing
to be experienced and enjoyed just up ahead.
And as we think of all such blessed sharing,

as we take up our daily walk to Bethlehem
where God shared himself with us,
we take time to think of others, those in danger
and distress, all those in desperate need,
those who face terrible decisions,
those with no possible decisions left to be made,
all those in whom the face of Christ
lies waiting to be recognized and welcomed.

Slow us down, O God, this Advent season.
Let us savor every sparkling winter sunrise,
every golden sunset. Let us claim again the grace
that shapes each moment of our days,
and let us live that love that leads us toward life,
that simplest, deepest, truest love of all,
the love we will discover in the stable among the straw.
All this we ask in the tender, gracious,
world-embracing name of the Bethlehem babe,
our Savior, Jesus. Amen.

Advent Invitation

Step into a four-Sabbath world
that begins with a whisper—
"Keep your eyes peeled"—
concludes with the cry of a child in the night,
a realm that is bounded by the fling of five candlelight,
the range of a quavering voice reading words
that sound old and familiar, yet strange,
full of wonder and wanting,
a domain hung with banners of purple,
decked with green, living branches,
and spangled with frost, touched by star-beam.
You will meet friendly beasts,
an Orient wisdom, and folk from the fields.
Whatever you do, you'll be changed just a bit,
your blood colder, or warmer, you'll see.
One more thing. There is danger here,
much to be risked, perhaps all to be won.
Now take a deep breath. Let's begin.

Going to Bethlehem

Four weeks to cross the continents
and oceans to a town that is transformed
by twenty centuries of troubled times.

Four weeks in which to travel down
the weary corridors, two thousand years
of looking back and looking forward.

Four weeks for tramping the harsh pathways
of the shopping malls trying to buy the one gift
that has never been for sale.

Four weeks to light four candles
in the sanctuary of the heart, and then
a fifth one to illuminate the heart of God.

Four weeks for learning mystery, for turning
darkness toward light, for yearning, day
by day, toward that burning flame of welcome
that kindles there within the waiting manger.

HANGING THE GREENS

We bring the outside in
this chill and waning season,
cut boughs and branches,
strands of light and living green,
and deck them all about the walls
and ledges of our houses, make believe
we fashion an enchanted forest glade
to frame our festive celebrations.

Evergreens, we call them,
though they bleed and die so soon,
in over-heated rooms. Yet that dying
lends a fragrance and a grace, foretells,
if we will heed, another time and space,
where tree and thorns, no longer green,
fulfil their cruel, necessary function
in the ever-greening of our wintered race.

Watch For It

We need to be reminded
to look forward at least once a year.
So much we spend in peering back
across an urgent shoulder in these fearful times,
leery in case old you-know-who is gaining on us.

Therefore, just when calendars are growing
weary of themselves—the tattered, dog-eared,
tail-end of the year—we name it, Advent,
dig out five candles and the holly wreath,
and kindle hope again, with orisons, chants, hymns,
ringing words of ancient expectation.

In the midst of which, from time to time,
eternity—in ordinary flesh, and blood, and bone—
takes shape, dons time, draws near.

Tuesday

How Many Miles to Bethlehem? I

The Departure

The people who walked in darkness
have seen a great light;
those who dwelt in a land of deep darkness,
on them has light shined

—Isaiah 9:2

And Mary said, "Behold I am the handmaid of the Lord;
let it be to me according to your word."

—Luke 1:38

It all brought back so many memories of departure. We were in Fenchurch Street Station, catching a train to take us out of London to stay with old friends in nearby Essex. We raced along the platform with our bags, clambered through the first available carriage door, stowed the luggage overhead, settled down, and opened the window just a crack. A few moments later, with the urgent slamming of the few doors remaining open and the shriek of the whistle from the guard, the train began to move, and we sank back into our seats with a sigh of relief and contentment. We were on our way—setting out.

It's still a magical moment, even after the passing of many years, a moment calling forth memories of those enormous steam locomotives with their puffing, gasping, and hissing, their chugging, clashing and clanking, as they labored to get under way, memories of childhood journeys that were always, no matter the circumstances—and in wartime Britain there were some difficult and unusual ones—always brimming with anticipation and hope. Setting out! As we set out for Bethlehem today, as we get under way once again after all the activity, the turmoil and testing of another year's passing, I want to pose one simple, vital question. Are we ready for departure?

One of the more fascinating sections of the daily newspaper for me these days, one of the sections I hardly ever skip over, is the obituary page. A favorite *New Yorker* cartoon shows a senior citizen, probably about my age, seated in an armchair scanning the obituary columns. In the thought balloons floating above his head one reads these words: "Five years older than I am." "Two years younger than I am." "Same age as I am . . ."

It's most likely all to do with getting older, and I realize I'm not alone in this, but there's something about those lives set out in newsprint columns there, their tragedies and triumphs, that helps me take a deeper look at my own life, at the way I spend my days and hours. And I wonder sometimes whether *they* were ready—how it must have been for them to be one moment in the midst of an active, productive, basically satisfying life, and the next to be at the departure point, to be thrust out into a journey about which we know so little and fear so much. Were they ready for departure? Are we ready to move on?

Some months ago I read a miraculous little book called, *The Diving Bell and The Butterfly*. In its one hundred or so pages Jean-Dominique Bauby describes what it was like for him to get ready. Struck down at age forty-three by a devastating stroke that left him a victim of what the medical world calls Locked-In Syndrome, Bauby was unable to move or to communicate in any way. The only controllable movement left to him was that of blinking his left eye—the other eye had to be sewn shut. Yet, by means of this, Bauby devised an entire alphabet of blinking, and was able to compose, with the help of a scribe, a most eloquent and elegant memoir: a reflection on his life, his love, his daily round in the hospital, his hope and his fear, his getting ready. *The Diving Bell and the Butterfly*.

The Diving Bell is Bauby's name for the machinery, all the apparatus of high-tech modern medicine that keeps him breathing, thinking, blinking. *The Butterfly*, on the other hand, is his mind and spirit, a spirit that floats free as the air, and explores both the wonder and the terror of creation. At the very end, reviewing the pages he has composed with his amanuensis, his translator, he looks back across what has been, and what will be, and closes with these words, "We must keep looking. I'll be off now."

Two days after the book was published Jean-Dominique Bauby's locked-in body finally gave up on him, and he died. But for all the tragedy, for all his relative youth and unfulfilled potential, he was ready. He had learned, through some severe, yet ultimately splendid mercy, what we all must learn—if not, pray God, in such a harsh and challenging way—and that is to look hard at life and death, all its grim reality, and then seek out the depth, the dimension of the sacred that lies in every instant of existence. Bauby had learned to so live in the present moment that, whatever the future, his life had known truth, had claimed integrity, had received and given love.

I stood in the shadows of Hexham Abbey. It has long been favorite spot of mine, up in the northern English borderlands. My cousin and aunt both lived close by, so I could usually manage to fit in a visit. Saint Wilfrid's chair there dates back to the year 674 or thereabouts. But this time, as I slipped through the old oak doors—the organist practicing a great Bach prelude for next morning's service—I was taken by the gaudy, painted panels all around the fourteenth-century pulpit. They dated from the time of the bubonic plague, the Black Death, and each one showed an individual human figure, a prince, a magistrate, a merchant, a soldier, a young maiden, accompanied by the ghastly, dancing shape of Death itself, its rag-wrapped skeleton reaching out to seize them for its own. The intriguing thing was, the more I tried to catch that dark, macabre figure, first with my eyes, then with the camera lens, the less I could see of it. The light, the radiant morning light, streaming into that darkened church through the towering east window, was striking those smooth, varnished panels in such a way, at just such an angle, that the figure of death was almost totally obscured, obscured by the light.

I was somewhat irritated by this—to tell the truth—and left the abbey frustrated by my inability to get a decent photograph. It was not until much later that I realized that, instead of a photograph, I had been granted a vision. I had glimpsed something of what the Word is trying to say to us this morning through Isaiah's words:

> The people who walked in darkness have seen a great light; those who dwelt in a land of deep darkness, on them has light shined.

The darkness is real, very real. Mortality, loneliness, futility, they are there, all about us, and in the lengthened vision of these early winter days we seem to see them more clearly than before. The darkness is real, but the light, that radiance that blocked and then transformed my vision, is even more real. And rather than fleeing the dark, rather than trying to create our own artificial glare of amusement, diversion, distraction, we must look into the shadows, face up to the reality, and discover there, right in the heart of darkness, the heart of God, that comes among us in Christ our Lord.

The astronomers tell us an intriguing thing about light: they maintain that if we would catch the brightest stars of winter, we must be prepared to rise well before the dawn and search them out against the almost perfect black of the December sky. So it is that, in this darkest season of the year, when all around seems gloomy, grim, and grey, our faith begins the Advent season, the church begins, even before the dawn, to turn toward the light, to prepare herself—lighting candles, hanging greens, singing songs, saying prayers, and cultivating charity and kindness—for the One who comes to dazzle our death-filled eyes with his own eternal brilliance, and to show us that light of life that the darkness cannot hold back nor will ever comprehend.

Setting out for Bethlehem. Are we ready to set off? Are we ready to sit loose to those ties, those habits and attachments, all those belongings that would hold us back, weigh down our days of travel? Are we ready to launch out again on the journey to the stable, and to the child who awaits us there with laughter, song, and sounds of great rejoicing? Are we ready?

≈

Walk close beside us, Lord. Be our companion and support when the way seems long and weary. Then bring us, in your own good time, to the stable and the stall, to the still point of the turning world, to the gift of life revealed as we can kneel and offer up our souls, ourselves, then worship and adore. Amen.

Wednesday

GREETING

Sooner than ever—or so it seems—
that time of year is here again,
time when there is so little time to do the well-worn,
needful things, selecting trees and garlands,
not to mention gifts—just where is that old address list
left on the back of one of last year's envelopes?—
a time when benedictions gather into heaps
with every morning's mail,
as friendships are renewed on slips
of cheerful colored-paper.
Anyway, here's wishing you some time,
time to kneel, at least,
within the cloistered chamber of the soul,
and say, or sing, or even weep, a word of peace
and promise, maybe praise. Whatever time we have,
that's what it's given for.

Advent Awakening

Just when you felt convinced
that the inevitable was already happening,
just when the utter daily-ness of every single thing
had finally persuaded you not to expect,
not even to look,
just when tomorrow
had completely forfeited its meaning
as distinct from everyday,
a melody of dancing was caught from far away,
one long sigh became transmuted in mid-air
into a gasp of sheer astonishment.
And now a word, He comes,
new whispered on December's wind,
melts grim-set lips to simple speech,
and song, and framing age-old salutations.

Advent—Opening Bell

Stepping out
into a season overstuffed
with every kind of expectation,
except the kind we pray about in church,
four weeks—give or take—of sales charts,
balance sheets, consumer confidence reports,
and pay checks spent before they hit the bank,
I fear that any word of a messiah's birth might bring
only a momentary dip in the Dow Jones,
the merest trace of jitters along Wall Street.

RE-PETITION

"Come again?" we ask,
meaning, "Please tell me one more time,
I didn't quite catch your message."
"Come again?"
Daily praying—without realizing it—
this earliest of all our invocations,
"Maranatha—Come Again!"

He does, of course, in daily bread
and Bibles, Sunday pulpits, tables too,
calls to love and duty, most especially
through this leaning forward season
when winter's coat of white moves
greening toward Bethlehem.
The word is, "Come again!"

Thursday

Looking for Christmas I
Looking for Something

Thou hast said, "Seek ye my face."
My heart says to Thee,
"Thy face, Lord, do I seek."
Hide not Thy face from me.

—Psalm 27:8

Watch therefore, for you do not know on what day your Lord is
coming.

—Matthew 24:42

These Advent days are days in which everyone seems to be looking for something. Perhaps it is the perfect gift for someone who has everything already, or it may be the ideal shape tree for that difficult corner of your living room. Is it a card with a message that seems personally selected for each of your two hundred most intimate friends, yet is also both ecological and economical? Or might you be searching for a place at which, or a person or persons with whom, to spend the holiday season? Perhaps your hunt is for that fruitcake recipe, so successful last year, those delightful new decorations put away so carefully you forgot just where you did put them, that totally unique experience which will make this Christmas truly unforgettable.

Is your search, perhaps, a more desperate one: a quest for a blessed infusion of cold, hard cash to beat back those grim tidings of great bills in the Christmas mails, or for a few additional hours in which to get every last thing done, or even for a little peace and quiet in which to pause and recall what Christmas is truly all about? Whatever it may be, in these early Advent days everyone does seem to be looking for something.

But this is hardly just the case in Advent. Is there anyone nowadays who does not know the regular frustration of mislaying some object, and then wasting precious moments, even hours and days, "looking for something"? I hope it's not the advancing years that bring it on, but somehow things, previously inanimate objects—keys, checkbooks, shopping lists, umbrellas—seem to be developing a habit of avoiding me of late, avoiding and/or evading me. Have you ever found yourself, for example, wondering what it was you forgot in the first place, trying to remember what it was you had been trying to remember? That's when you know you have a problem.

Literature too—that rich treasury of story, saga, and fable—is filled with searches. From the ancient quest of Gilgamesh through the sagas of the Norsemen, King Arthur and the Grail, the rings of Tolkien, and of Wagner, all the way to the science-fiction fables of tomorrow—and all of them looking, looking for something.

The scientific community nowadays with its microscopes and telescopes, its atom smashers and colliders, shares this same understanding of itself as engaging in a continuing search, a search for something yet to be discovered—the secret of life, the cure for cancer, the source of unlimited energy, the outermost limits of the universe, the innermost, most elemental core from which all other building blocks of being are constructed. And all of them, all of us, are looking for something. In fact one might reasonably summarize the status, the basic condition of this entire human race, in just these three words. Whether it be the pot of gold at the end of the rainbow, the fountain of youth, or that glorious city of God described in the Scriptures, to be human is to be *looking for something.*

What is it then that we are looking for, beneath all these secondary quests, these intermediate investigations? What is it *you* are looking for? Are you looking for a home, a place you used to know and cherish, but which only now exists as a coziness and warmth, a belonging, back at the furthest reaches of the memory? Are you looking for a home?

Are you looking for prosperity? Not, perhaps, ten million dollars, but sufficient financial resources so you can break away from the monthly scraping and hoping over the checking account, afford the occasional something that is shiny, soft, and absolutely foolish, for yourself, and for those you love?

Are you looking for recognition, yearning for people to know you, who you are and how you are? (A bore has been defined as someone who, when you ask him how he is, tells you.) Are you looking for recognition?

Are you looking for adventure, something, anything, to break up the murderous monotonies of daily bread and then to bed, five, six, seven days a week? Are you looking for adventure?

Could it be health you are after, a confidence in your own well-being, so that you can make it over the hurdles, through the lurking pitfalls of life and, if not defeat that last enemy, at least die fulfilled at a ripe old age?

Are you looking for peace, peace in the world of course, but more than that, peace within? Do you seek peace with your own self, so that you can forgive yourself, accept yourself, even begin actually to be yourself, instead of the person you think others expect you to be?

Are you looking for love, that giving which is also, and uniquely a receiving, a receiving of another self, a beloved self, and then the receiving of your own self back again, refreshed, restored, renewed by the tenderness and concern, the laughter and hope, the fresh vision of yourself caught in someone else's eyes and dreams? Are you looking, still looking, for love?

Then come with me to Bethlehem. Come, all who are seeking for any of the above to where we will find, if not the end of our searching, at least a new and true beginning, a key with which to open doors, a clue by which to solve life's mysteries, a child in whose humble, innocent, and lovely birth we can find ourselves reborn. Come, take the road to Bethlehem this December morning, set out again upon this age-old, brand-new journey, and let us look for something, look for Christmas together throughout this Advent season.

President Howard Lowry of The College of Wooster used to describe in his freshman classes a boyhood camping trip into the deep caves of Kentucky. Far, far back, at last, among the stalactites and stalagmites, crawling along a narrow ledge with a guide and a few bold friends, they turned a corner and came upon a wall covered with initials and names of other campers, other intrepid explorers who had preceded them in years past. And there, by the dim, smoky light of a lantern, he discovered with a thrill his own father's name, carved years before on a similar expedition.

The Christian church in our time—an era shadowed by terror, crime, corruption, and despair—today's community of believers can be seen like that daring group, a search party, explorers risking the deeper, often darker facets of life to look for something. We have provisions for the journey, simple bread and royal wine to sustain the soul. We have our guide in him whose name we bear as Christians, whose wounded feet have marked the way ahead. We have our lantern shining-bright within the pages of our ancient, holy book. So let us pray that, as we search together, we too may turn that final corner, may reach out and trace our Father's name; and thus know the search is ended, the lost is found, and we are home, and we are welcomed within our Father's house, forever and forever.

∾

You are the Way, Lord Christ. Lead us, in our quest, to ourselves and then beyond. You are the Truth, Lord Christ. Teach us to know you, and thus to know ourselves in you. You are the Life, Lord Christ. So bring your Life to birth in us this Advent, until we come to kneel and to adore, to give ourselves, and lose ourselves, and find ourselves in you. Amen.

Friday

ANTICIPATION?

Looking forward comes more readily
to folk whose here and now is not so God-Almighty
crammed with all this getting and maintaining.
Even these Advent calendars and candles
can soon become another detour,
distracting from the blessed emptiness
that filled the Virgin's Womb.

Is there a sacral stripping
can purge, prepare, accommodate,
make spare and elemental room for whatever
holy mystery there is to come?
Or will this omnipresent fatness
swallow up, consume, devour all keen anticipation,
transform our expectation into old, habitual doom.

Seasonings

The gentle, sure, progression
of four candled Sabbaths toward the stable,
those forty, purple-proving days to find a way
from winter into spring, scarlet-flamed Pentecost,
white, and shining-bright Epiphany,
such feastings, fasts, and festivals—
this numbering and naming of the days and weeks—
played little or no part within the Calvinistic calendar
of my Scottish boyhood, kirk-encapsulated years.
"All Catholic mumbo-jumbo . . . hocus-pocus,"
was the general, grim, self-satisfied consensus.
Just show me, if you can,
where you will find this in the Bible.

Even so does eager zeal,
and dry, unliberated intellect,
strip life away from life,
drastically diminish holy wonder,
and, in the austere name of barren truth,
leave days and seasons, faith itself, impoverished.

EARLY ADVENT

This purple takes a bit of getting used to,
ditto candles, wreaths and greens,
plus greeting cards arriving in the mail.
Surely it's not that time again already . . .
time to get ready, as so many times before,
prepared to greet the coming of that One who,
despite all our days and years of solemn expectation,
never fails to surprise,
to advent in the most unsuitable of venues,
dazzle with tears of memory, loss, regret,
the mad-yet-mending impulses of tenderness,
faint, yet still fair, fragrances of future hope,
then leave behind a lingering glimpse
of warm, mid-winter welcomes yet to be.

ADVENT PREMONITION

And so it all begins again,
the candles and the purple cloths,
the holly and the ivy, the tree to be set up,
cards to sign and seal, to stamp and mail,
those certain, blessed songs to sing, and the *un*certain too.
We call it "getting ready," as if we were ever ready
for whatever it is that's ripening up ahead.
Fact is, it will surprise us, shock us,
knock our socks off, turn us inside out.
We have been warned.

In the meantime, where did we put away
those golden Christmas bells that looked
so perfect over the front door last year?

Saturday

GIFTS OF ADVENT I

Promise

Now when these things begin to take place, look up and raise your head, because your redemption is drawing near.

—LUKE 21:28

In the midst of a presidential election season a young schoolboy called Brad, in Reading, Pennsylvania, composed the following essay:

> If I were Presdent . . . If I were Presdent I would wish for a better world. And no guns or wars. NO litter. And everybody would be friends. And nobody would lie. No body would eat brussel sprouts or zewckeine.

What a platform! What a vision! Peace, no litter, no crooks, and NO vegetables either. Way to go, young man!

There is more involved here, however, than smiles at a youngster's unsophisticated view of the world. What Brad is doing here is presenting a promise, a vision, his personal vision of the future. And more than anything else, in these shadowed, yet expectant days, we need such visions. Is this not, in fact, a major part of the perennial magic of these days and weeks before Christmas? They give us something to look forward to: they give us that essential gift, the gift of promise.

"Where there is no vision, the people perish," warns the book of Proverbs 29:18 (KJV). And in a host of situations nowadays this would appear to be the case. Ask the nurses and attendants in our nursing homes and hospitals and they will tell you that the elderly and frail, even the terminally ill, will hold out, hang on to life for holidays, birthdays, weddings, those major family occasions; but afterwards, when there is nothing left to look forward to, they slip away.

Some years ago now Mhairi, my wife, and I—ourselves first-generation immigrants—visited Ellis Island and its splendidly renovated Immigration Museum. And there, shining through all those sepia-toned photographs, still lingering among the displays of family belongings and relics, resonant in the scratchy, recorded voices from long ago, we could not help but sense the presence of a vast promise, the living, breathing, almost reach-out-and-touch-able vision that this nation represented to the millions who came here. It was Nietzsche, that great challenger of visions, who wrote: He who has a why to live for can bear with almost any how.[2] It seems that we human beings are built for, designed and engineered to run on, hope. It is as vital, as essential to the soul, as oxygen is to the blood. We require, we absolutely need to have, a promise.

As soon as one says this, however, one has to concede that there are promises, and then there are promises. One of the most damning critiques of religion over the centuries has been that it has catered to this universal need by holding out false promises, by cultivating empty hopes. "Pie in the sky religion" these critics have dubbed it, when churches seek to pacify poor and oppressed peoples, to make needy folk content with their lot, by holding out the promised consolation of an eternal reward awaiting them in heaven. Yet it seems to me that the false promises *we* are faced with, the delusory visions *we* need to worry about in our day and age, have more to do with this present life than with any future realm. As travel writer Rick Steves, quoted recently in *Christian Century* magazine, points out,

> While aristocracy-controlled religion was the opiate of the masses back then, corporate-controlled media is the opiate of the masses today.[3]

2. Nietzsche, *Twilight of the Idols*, maxim and arrow 12.
3. Steves, "Travel Writer."

Perhaps nowadays we ought to be denouncing, not "Pies in the Sky When we Die," but "Pies in the Media," "Pies in the Lottery and Stock Market," "Pies in all the cheap escapes and empty satisfactions thrust before us every day."

Pulitzer Prize winning journalist and sage James Reston wrote of our time as one in which people confuse the pursuit of happiness with the pursuit of pleasure. Reston saw our unnamed but universally agreed upon philosophy as one that encourages folk to seek what we used to call salvation in the endless accumulation of material wealth, one which leads people to build their hopes, their vision of future bliss, around a winning lottery ticket, a lucky number at Las Vegas. Surely it could be argued that, just like those religious "Pies in the Sky Bye and Bye," this here-and-now secular promise—of instant and unimaginable wealth, success, satisfaction, sex appeal—can also have the effect of pacifying the needy and oppressed, of distracting all kinds of people from the captivities they face in daily life.

We need a promise; we human beings must have something to hope for. Yet so much of what we do actually pin our hopes upon is inadequate at best, sheer foolishness at worst. What then? Perhaps, at last, we are ready for the genuine promise, the authentic vision of Advent. This is a different kind of promise: more elusive, but also more enduring. It is a promise of something that will always be beyond us, yet somehow can, at the same time, be within us; something that is within our reach—we can stretch out and touch it—yet is far beyond our grasp—we can never possess it or control it. This is not something we will ever achieve by our own individual efforts. Rather it is something which we can only *receive* in simple openness, faithfulness, and trust.

I cherish all those Old Testament prophecies of the coming of Messiah that we read at this time of year. They are so varied, so mysterious, so rich with enigma, possibility, and promise. Isaiah sings of one who is gentle and meek, "a bruised reed he will not break, a dimly burning wick he will not quench . . ." yet one who will establish universal justice, feed the hungry, free the captives, do away with poverty forever (42:3–4). Malachi has The Promised

One coming in a fury of judgment, a purifying fire (3:2–3). Hosea sings of a lovely garden, "I will be as the dew to Israel; he shall blossom as the lily, he shall strike root as the poplar . . . his beauty shall be like the olive, and his fragrance like Lebanon" (14:5–6). Crazy old Balaam foresees a star coming forth out of Jacob, a scepter arising out of Israel (Num 24:17). And Jacob on his deathbed blesses his sons with the mysterious promise of Shiloh who is to come (Gen 49:10). Marvelous words they are, musical words, words that conjure hope and expectation, a vision of the future that is beyond precise and specific definition, yet is all the more powerful because of that reality.

They sing to us, these ancient seers, of trust in God, the God who holds all history in his hands. And the fascinating thing is that, as they present these hopes, as they paint these varied, multifaceted visions of the future, they do not spell out what we must do in order to get there. There are no detailed guidelines or programs, few, if any, itineraries for the journey toward the heavenly city. What they do tell us, one and all, is to be ready, to watch and pray, to make straight in the desert of our own lives and times a highway for our God.

Isn't that what we're ultimately put here for, after all—right at the heart of these amazingly creative, yet murderously violent times—to seek out, and then hold up a different vision, to show forth, make clear, an alternative to the gloss, the evanescent fluff this constantly consuming society of ours pours forth in such calculated abundance?

Not much of a contest really, or so it would seem, all the flash and power of the internet, the glossy magazines, the bulk mailings and the media, over against our individual lives, our modest little Sunday morning clusters. And yet the message of this season centers around just such a contest: a flickering candle in the looming, almost overwhelming dark, a fragile reed that bends before the gale but never breaks, a tender child, as full of promise today as he was two thousand years ago, an infant whose tiny, apparently powerless hands embraced the hopes and fears of all the world, still hold them tight today.

Advent is the season for promise. There are the promises of God that are fulfilled, and then renewed, in that humble manger birth. But there are also promises evoked in response, promises on our part that are called for in this season. Therefore, by the welcome we extend to all we meet, of whatever race, economic level, sexual orientation, by the generosity we extend to those in cruel want these wintered days, by the witness we bear to those in power against injustice and inequality, we must renew our own commitment to this vision—the vision of the prophets and of the Christ child—and work toward a world built on promise not on fear, built on hope and not the counsels of despair.

Above all we must claim this Advent gift of promise. The promise of our God to be faithful if we will only trust, to be with us in our struggles and trials no matter the odds, and in the child of Bethlehem—Immanuel—God with us—to take our yearning, hurting, ever hoping hearts and hold them, heal them, mold them, grant them peace. That is the promise that God gives us in this season. That is the gift of Advent.

∼

Lord, in all the looking forward, all the expectation of this season, turn our hearts toward your coming. Teach us to watch for that greatest gift of all: your presence, your grace, your vision of the kingdom yet to come. Amen.

Advent Week Two

Sunday

SOMETHING FOR CHRISTMAS II
Something Worth Waiting For

Wait for the Lord; be strong and let your heart take courage
yea, wait for the Lord!

—PSALM 27:14

If it seem slow, wait for it; it will surely come, it will not delay.

—HABAKKUK 2:3

. . . for the creation waits with eager longing for the revealing of the
sons of God.

—ROMANS 8:19

Some months ago I began yet another course of physical therapy; things tend to develop that way when you reach what are
dubiously called "the golden years." As I sat there waiting . . . waiting . . . waiting for my name to be called, my bored and weary brain
flipped back to another such occasion, several years before, the
first time, as I recall, that I had actually undergone such treatment.
The therapy, on both occasions had been prescribed for shoulder
pain, due to wear and tear on something known as the rotator
cuff, a condition I had thought afflicted only major league baseball
pitchers. There can be, for some, a certain satisfaction, something
vaguely "jock-ish" about such therapy and, I must confess, I did
relish at first this imaginary mini-communion with such legendary sporting figures as Sandy Koufax, Steve Carlton, and Roger
Clemens. But not for long.

They led me into a tiny room, laid me out, half-naked, on a narrow bed, and tucked ice packs around each shivering shoulder. Then they turned the light out and abandoned me. The intriguing thing was that I quickly got used to the cold; what really bothered me was having to lie there for fifteen minutes and do absolutely nothing. In fact, after that initial experience, I made sure I took a book or magazine along and insisted that they leave the light on. I just could not afford the time to simply lie there and be healed.

And here we are in Advent once again, a season when, of all year long, time seems to be most precious, and in most short supply. How many shopping days are left, not to mention mailing days, baking days, cleaning days, decorating days, partying days? The countdown has been off and running for some time now and the momentum is becoming irresistible, sweeping people into the frantic pace, the frenetic race of getting ready, getting ready to be happy at Christmas.

Yet, in contrast with this scene in the secular world, these weeks that we Christians traditionally call Advent are all about waiting, about patience, about trusting, not in our own energies and organization to get everything done, but in the Lord to bring his happiness to earth for us at Christmas. And we are not, at least I am not—as I learned at that therapist's office—much good anymore at waiting.

We exist nowadays in an instant, on-demand society, where the microwave takes far too long, and after more than twenty seconds in an elevator we start pressing buttons to get the door to close and get on with it. Why wait for a thing to be repaired, we reason, when it's just about as cheap to buy a new one? Why wait in long and tedious lines at the store, when you can order everything online? Why wait until you can afford it to enjoy the newest toy, the latest electronic gadget, your winter cruise in the sun, when you can put it on plastic and worry about it later? We are not very good anymore at waiting.

Another waiting experience I have been undergoing of late, in this season of traveling and visiting, has been that of waiting for a train. I'm sure many who read these words have sat, as I have, in one of those splendid old center-city railroad stations, New York's majestic Grand Central, for example, or Philadelphia's elegant 30th Street Station, waiting for the Metro-liner. After a while it becomes not all that difficult to set aside the fussing and fuming at those repetitive security announcements, the dreary details of scheduling glitches and delays, to lay aside the newspaper, and simply to wait, and to be alive in that waiting.

You can look around and up at the spectacular building, recalling a time when folk believed it was important to take time—time enough to build something that will stand the test of time. You can take the time, in waiting, to survey the fascinating parade of people passing by—the soldier, in combat fatigues, preparing for who knows what, who knows where, disheveled college students on their wanderings to and fro, a young mother struggling with suitcases and two adorable little girls, Brooks Brothers-suited business types complete with laptops, smartphones, and *Wall Street Journals*. Then there are the homeless, aimless, lost—begging handouts in a routinely hopeless manner.

On just such a trip, to New York City, I toured a visiting exhibit of Dutch Masters at my favorite museum, the Frick, alongside Central Park. Searching in vain for a spot to sit and reflect on those miraculous Rembrandts and Vermeers, I was reminded of instructions issued by a guide at Florence's famed Uffizi Galleries. "Don't stop to look at anything," she told her charges, "or you won't have time to see everything." A story that is certainly worth a smile, but also a telling illustration of the way we go through our days, so eager to get everything done, to squeeze everything possible in, that we never have time to stop, look, listen, and thus find ourselves in the timeless presence of God.

Waiting can be a gift, if we are ready to receive it, a gift of time—unscheduled, unorganized, wide-open time—time in which to be and to see, to listen and to hear, to become aware of where we are, and how we are, and who we really are. *Carpe Diem*—"Seize the day"—an ancient Latin motto revived some years ago in that fascinating movie, *Dead Poets' Society*. Yet in some ways we have become far too good at *seizing* the day, at grasping each and every passing hour by the scruff of the neck and compelling it to pay off in productive and profitable activity. Might it be that we need a new motto: *Suscipe Diem*—accept the day, receive the day, explore, even *embrace* the day? Above all, treat the day gently and with reverence, with high expectation and a steady, quiet hope. Waiting can teach us that.

During my formative years in Scotland my father was a baker. Last thing at night he would prepare the dough for the next morning's breakfast rolls, mixing, pounding, kneading the ingredients into a heavy, solid mass. This he would drop with a thud to the foot of a great wooden barrel and, tearing off a piece of yeast would toss it in on top. Then, covering the whole thing with a damp cloth, he would retire for the night. Long before dawn he would rise to a miraculous tub, filled to overflowing with airy, fluffy dough all ready for the oven, ready to be transformed into the crispest, brownest, best rolls in town. Then along came the newest invention from America; "Flying Dough," they called it. No more late nights and early risings. The dough rose almost instantly. But those rolls never tasted quite the same.

The best things we know have to be waited for; the most important things in life—wisdom, experience, special skills, and love, that above all,—the most important things we know require, *demand* our patience. They have their own unique timetable, and we have to let them take the time they need, *all* the time they need. "You can't make the grass grow by pulling on it," as they used to say when I was a boy back in Yorkshire. And it still takes just about nine months to create a healthy baby.

One more thing about waiting, and about time . . . it can be fatal. Time can be fatal. Several years ago, in a little cathedral town in south-central France, Mhairi, my wife, and I bought a sundial. It's a strange old plaque with zodiac signs and a lion's head, but the thing that caught my fancy, stopped me dead in my tracks, was the Latin inscription: *Vulnerant Omnes Ultima Necat* which means, in speaking of the passing hours, "They all wound. The last one kills." This gift of time we have received is a fleeting gift: it comes with no guarantees, no manufacturer's warranty—five years, 50,000 miles. Time is undeniably, and inevitably, limited.

In my now almost fifty years of ordained ministry I have spent considerable time with those who know this all too well, folk—friends, many of them—who have been informed that their days are numbered, advised to prepare for the end. And what never ceases to amaze is not the fear or the pain—they are there, of course, and cannot be denied—but the grace, sheer grace, with which most such individuals live out their days, even down to the end, a grace that says to you and me, "Take time, take *your* time, claim it as your own, even as it claims you, and live it—every single day of it—as the gift it truly is."

What we do indisputably have is today, this very day, a time to get ready, time to take time, time to discover the presence of God waiting for us, not just far off at the end of time, not even just in that manger scene Christians all over the world will celebrate a couple of weeks from now, but right here, right now, wherever you happen to be reading these words, in those whom you love and even those you fear or despise, in gardens and galleries, pastures and police stations, in every blessed and even cursed moment, the presence and the grace of God are there to be discovered, if we will only take our time.

Some four hundred years ago an Italian monk, Fra Giovanni Giocondo, wrote this greeting as a Christmas gift to a little girl, a child he had been tutoring. The monk and his young pupil are long gone, but if we can learn to wait for Christmas, his gift lives on to bless us on our way.

> There is nothing I can give, that you do not already have.
> But there is much that, while I cannot give, you can take.
>   No heaven can come to us unless our hearts find rest in it today. Take Heaven.
>   No peace lies in the future which is not hidden in this present instant. Take Peace.
>   The gloom of the world is but a shadow; behind it, yet within our reach, is joy. Take Joy.

And so, Contessina, I greet you with the prayer that for you, now, this Christmas season, and forever, the day breaks and the shadows flee away.[1]

~

Teach us to await your coming, Lord, in a calm and expectant awareness, that when you speak, we might respond; when you act, we might join you in that action; when you are born among us, we might worship and adore. Amen.

1. Giocondo, *A Letter*, n.p.

Monday

A Prayer for Hope in Advent

O God, the source and goal of all our hoping,
in a time of diminishing hope and dwindling faith,
a time when people can see little that spells promise
and so much that seems to spell disaster,
a time when our nation's founding vision
of community and trust has faded
to a disillusioned sense of resentment
and fear of one another,
Lord God, in these darkened days of early winter
we come before you in search of light.

Preserve us, as communities of faith,
from contention and division against one another.
When we disagree about solutions to problems,
or even about the problems themselves,
teach us how to disagree, yet to remain
rooted deep within your underlying love,
sheltered together beneath your over-arching grace.
Guide us to seek and find your truth in everyone we meet.
Lead us to that light that shone in Bethlehem long ago,
a light that led the poorest of the poor,
the humble shepherds,
and those kings bearing their royal gifts
of power, wealth and privilege,
to kneel beside the manger and to offer all they had,
all they were, before the mystery of birth
revealed in Christ our Lord.

You know our riches and our poverty, Lord God.
You know the emptiness and the yearnings,
the promises unmet, dreams unfulfilled,
affections unexpressed, that fill our days with shadows.
You see the milling throngs this time of year,
jamming the streets, crowding sidewalks and stores,
wandering, wondering, seeking to purchase
that one gift which has never been for sale,
the gift you freely offer of new life with destiny
and purpose, of new hope in community and trust,
of new and never ending love discovered in the act
of reaching out to give oneself away.

Move among us, Lord,
with your healing and forgiving grace,
just as you moved among those crowds so long ago.
Help us to recognize your living presence
in the simplest acts of kindness, words of welcome,
gestures of affection and goodwill.
Warm our hearts again toward one another.
And lift our eyes above these artificial stars
to the eternal glory of the heavens,
the evident joy of your creation,
the deep-down, dearest splendor of your grace
in all that is, ever has been, ever shall be.

Hear our prayers of compassion
for all who bear the cross of suffering,
the ever-present burdens of loneliness, despair, and grief,
the fear of death, the fear of life, the fear of love
that yet can turn, transform, all death to life in you.
May they know your healing presence, may they sense
the loving-kindness of your gentle, powerful touch.

Finally, O Lord, grant us
an Advent foretaste of the joy that is to come.
As little children anticipate the unwrapping of gifts
beneath the tree and know a glee that can scarce be contained,
so let our lives show forth the hope that is in them,
the faith we have in you, the caring we bear for one another.
Teach us to shine among the lights of this season
so that, like tall and graceful candles
we might bring an inner radiance to all we meet.
And when the hour strikes, the darkness lifts,
the infant's cry is heard again across this waiting world,
then grant us the humility to kneel and to adore.

All this we pray, with glad thanksgiving,
through the One who came, who comes,
who is to come. Amen.

THAT TIME AGAIN . . .

time to begin to look forward,
counting the weeks and the days
on the way to that—O, so familiar—surprise,
when all you have met down the years—
yes, the sad and glad, all foul and fair—
is un-parceled right there at the foot of the tree
and you discover what you always had hoped,
hardly dared—despite fear, those random glimpses
of despair—that life ends, as it started, in gentleness,
tenderest touch across the cheek, soft, smooth blanket,
and warm, full breast, the fond, embracing presence
of all you have ever held dear.

KALEIDOSCOPING CHRISTMAS

Approaching once again
    these holy days of high nativity,
        astounded at the mad accelerating
            pace of their return,
        the scanning eye is taken
    by a fleeting, fragmentary quality
in all that must take place.
    The steady, measured countdown of tradition,
        tracing the rich liturgical processing
            of the Advent days is, at best,
                a wistful hope, a plan adopted late
            in dull November which itself becomes
        drawn up into the tight kaleidoscope
    of hastening events.
It all seems to boil down
    to the fitting of things in,
        the insertion into almost non-
            existent spaces in the daily round
        of moments of potential magic,
    instants when the presence of eternity
can be recognized, acknowledged and accepted—
    like some glazed-eyed distance runner,
        seizing a taste of fruit juice without
            breaking stride. The fascination lies
                in what those angled mirrors set within
            the hollow tube are able to achieve,
        arranging all the odd and foolish juxtaposings
    of these days—both the mundane and the marvelous
into a new and startling pattern that displays relationships,
    pure possibility, a rare, demanding beauty.
        O, bless the hand that shakes and turns,
            sets with grace against the hungry,
        frantic eye this vision of
    the radiance of randomness.

TIME TO BE CAREFUL

since you never know
just when, and where, and how
it might be manifest. Watch children
and the rich in years, those winter birds
that wait with us through bitter months.
Renew the flame of quiet contemplation.
Dig out the old books and the songs
that fed you long ago, back when
the soul was tender toward mystery
and holiness. Above all else
be careful about care, so that,
in the rush of doing things for others,
you avoid spending all your time on things,
not on the others. That way lies
barrenness, and Herod's hasty sword.

Tuesday

How Many Miles to Bethlehem? II
The Company

The wolf shall dwell with the lamb, and the leopard shall lie down with the kid, and the calf and the lion and the fatling together, and a little child shall lead them.

—ISAIAH 11:6

A solitary couple are silhouetted against a darkening winter sky. The man, tall, robed, weary, walks ahead, leaning on his staff, and leading with his other hand a donkey, upon which sits a young woman, also robed, also weary, a graceful young woman, who bears a ring of light circled about her head. A classic scene, depicted on Christmas cards, in art galleries, deep in our imaginations. A solitary couple making that long journey up to Bethlehem alone, and at the worst time of the year.

Appealing as this familiar scene may be, it is a most unlikely one, and may even be completely inaccurate. People, particularly couples expecting their first child, did not travel the countryside alone in those days. The roads were rough, dangerous, marked by steep and twisting bends and narrow gorges where isolated travelers were easy prey for bandits and robbers. People traveled, when they had to, in larger groupings, companies, or caravans.

Furthermore, Bethlehem, being on the main route to Jerusalem, the capital, and also the sole registration point for all descendants of King David, must have been the destination for a motley horde of citizens, soldiers, merchants, scholars, beggars, tax collectors, and the like. Do we not read that because of just such a multitude all of the inns in town were packed to capacity? Picturesque as that solitary couple might seem, we can be fairly certain that, for security if for no other reason, Joseph and Mary traveled among a host of companions on that first Advent journey.

As we retrace that ancient route these Advent mornings, as we ask ourselves once again, *How Many Miles to Bethlehem?* the question arises of the fellowship we find ourselves among, the company we keep along the way. For, just as Mary and Joseph did, we too find ourselves surrounded by a host of fellow travelers, fellow pilgrims on this path toward the manger. Let's look around for a moment, check out who's walking with us, maybe even recognize a few of them as we make our way together.

First, let me propose, we walk among the company of memory, that treasured company of tradition, heritage, and the legacy of the past. The writer of the Epistle to the Hebrews reminds those earliest believers of the host—he describes them as a veritable cloud—of unseen witnesses, now dead and gone, who yet surround their pilgrimage, who move with them, and with us too, toward the sacred days ahead. "And all these," he writes, "though well attested by their faith, did not receive what was promised, since God had foreseen something better for us, that apart from us they should not be made perfect" (Heb 11:39-40).

Surely this season would be incomplete, left stark and sadly depleted, if it were cut off from all the accompaniments of the richly savored past. Where would Christmas be without the legends of Saint Nicholas, the Magi, Good King Wenceslas, and Amahl, without the soaring melodies and counterpoints of Handel, Bach, The Oxford Book of Carols, without the wondrous fictions—truer to life than life itself—of Charles Dickens and Leo Tolstoy? Even those old, beloved movies, *Miracle on 34th Street* and *It's a Wonderful Life*, have their part to play, along with the rosy, cozy, afterglow of idyllic winter scenes by Currier and Ives?

Included also in this company of memory there are those of whom our Scriptures would remind us. If we look back down the line of pilgrims far enough we will catch sight of faithful Father Abraham himself, who set out upon this journey forty centuries before us. And Moses walks there, giver of the Law, Elijah of the still, small voice, Isaiah, messenger of light in darkness, John the Baptist, with his strange desert garb of camel skins, his blazing eyes.

And here comes Augustine, Friar Aquinas too, Emperor Charlemagne, and Luther—old Brother Martin—assuring us that if we had actually been there in that messy cattle stall we would not have been kneeling, but holding our noses, muttering, "Tut-tut!" and passing swiftly by on the other side.

There is our personal looking back as well—those fondly cherished memories of thirty, forty years ago and more—back to a time when we first glimpsed, beyond the tinsel and the tree, through to the wonder, magic, marvel of it all, back also to all those who stood about us then, parents, grandparents, brothers, sisters, uncles, cousins, aunts, all those whose presence and whose love, however difficult and at times convoluted, lit the flame, kindled the warmth, that has never quite gone out. For they too walk beside us on this road, this ancient highway, that leads us on toward *Immanuel*—God with us. As we pause a moment and remember, we recall them, call them back, and bid them welcome to this company we keep. Yes, we walk among the company of memory as we make our pilgrim way to Bethlehem.

There is also here beside us on this busy Bethlehem road, the company of today, of this present here-and-now. There are the throngs who press against us on the city streets, in the markets, malls, and shops. There are the worshippers who sing and pray beside us in the pews. There is the network of the internet, neighbors, acquaintances, associates, whose words and thoughts impinge upon our everyday whether we value them or not. Those cards arriving daily in the mails recall this company we stand in, cards from around the world, from distant cousins, relations, friends, in far-off Europe, Africa, Asia. We move together at this time in search of one who is to come.

Farther afield even than these, we travel in the company of fellow believers in China, Pakistan, the Middle East, lands where to believe as we do, to dare to kneel before the manger, can cost your job, your home, your family, even your life—all those we learn of in the news, who seek only a spot to lay their heads, a crumb of bread, clean drinking water for their children, a basic human gesture that speaks tenderness and hope; we walk in such a company today. And if we do not, should we prove unwilling to join this limping, halting throng, then we do not walk the way at all, because it was to these and such as these that Jesus joined himself by being born in bleak and bitter poverty.

Then there are those who, even while they walk, dispute and disagree with us, those who would claim that we do not belong, that we have no place beside them in this pilgrimage. Yet somehow we must learn to walk with them, talk with them, and even, for that's finally what this journey is about, care for them. How marvelous it is—as one of my oldest, dearest parishioners used to chuckle to me, "Isn't God something, the way he arranges things."

A company of memory, a company of the present, and third, we walk within a company of the future, the company of tomorrow. Twenty-five centuries ago, in a time of despair, exile, and persecution, Isaiah the prophet sang of days that were, still are, yet to come.

> The wolf shall dwell with the lamb, and the leopard shall lie down with the kid, and the calf, and the lion, and the fatling together, and a little child shall lead them (Isa 11:6).

How could Isaiah dare to say that? No one alone, in such harsh circumstances of slavery and deprivation, no solitary individual could have conjured up that kind of vision. It would have been too ironic, too unattainable, too cruel. It would have sounded like utter madness. Only God, God who holds the future in his hands, could hold out such a promise, such a hope.

That promise is still ours today. That's what this Advent season is for, not shopping-days-till-Christmas, but the renewal, the recharging of our dreams, the restoration of our vision of the kingdom yet to be. In this time of deepest darkness, as the year draws in toward its longest night, we Christians set out upon a journey and cast our eyes, our thoughts, our spirits far ahead toward that promise of a fuller, finer, truer time to come, when peace shall be established, justice become our daily way of life, God's grace shall bind all peoples, all creation into one, and a little child shall lead them.

Remembrance, then, commitment, and true hope—the generations long departed, yet still marching in our blood, our souls, within the eternal host of God—the present bonds and ties of affection, need and fellowship that bind us all together in this hour—the generations yet unborn, who live within our genes, within our dreams, who trust somehow that we will pass along to them a future that is still livable. And in and through all this the one who is both source and goal, who sends us on our way and guides us home rejoicing, the one who in the candlelight, the manger birth, the infant's cry has come, still comes, will come again to join us, and to greet us all together at journey's end.

∼

Travel with us, Lord, and keep us mindful of all who walk this road beside us. Travel with us, Lord, lest we forget our heritage, forsake the needy, forfeit the future you have prepared. Even so, bind us in the community of creation, and bring us to the stillness at the center, the sacred at the heart. Amen.

Wednesday

ADVENT CANDLES

In
stant
glare
from
the
light switch declares
them redundant for
seeing, a poor yet
expensive procedure
to scare off the dark.
But only a candle can
incense the air for our
viewing, can kindle it,
color it, bend it, for
atmosphere blend a spare
shadow or two, can flicker
and flare with a mood for
each moment and season,
prepare the bleak night of
our winter for mystery, magic-past-reason,
the suddenly shimmering vision that
brings us to birth.

CHRISTMAS MAIL

I count them surreptitiously—
knowing she really doesn't think it right—
announce the final total only in a whisper
to myself, you see, I too do not approve,
would not admit to anyone such pitiful,
pathetic calculation. What kind of fool
would poll his friendships, success, even
Christmas spirit, according to the tally
of these pretty, colored cards?

And yet—setting arithmetic aside—
there is a buried treasure concealed
somewhere underneath these cardboard,
crass, commercial symbols,
the trace of an insistent, still more deep
reality, that impels me, year after calculating year,
to send abroad at least a scribbled/heartfelt word or two,
seeking to bind and weave fond memory
into the rich-embroidered tapestry of future hope.

Lux plus Veritas

We try to drive the dark away this shining season,
string twining cords around our shrubs and trees,
doors, windows, porches too, bedeck our shadowed world
with myriad winking, blinking, points of multi-colored light.
All this to stretch the dwindling daylight out,
limit the chill domain of winter's night.

"It makes the holidays more bright . . ." we tell ourselves,
forgetting that this stable cave we celebrate
was lighted by, at most, one of those tiny, clay oil lamps;
that the clear radiance that streamed above, around,
beyond that battered-blessed manger drew from
deep within the all-surrounding dark.

Even so, one sparkling island night in Maine, I introduced
our first granddaughter, raised in illuminated New York City,
to the black-velvet-spread celestial of The Milky Way.
Her sheer astonishment made crystal clear
that we must claim our darkness too,
if we would glimpse the glory of the elemental light.

Advent Haiku

Before we know it
through purple cloths and candles
Bethlehem beckons.

                                    To wait and wonder
                                    if the one who is to come
                                    will bear surprises.

Four candles
to illuminate the dark
of the year, the cave, the soul.

Thursday

LOOKING FOR CHRISTMAS II
Looking Forward For Christmas

And what I say to you I say to all: "Watch."

—MARK 13:37

This Advent season seems to be pervaded by that tantalizing feeling we call anticipation. There is, for example, that lovingly selected gift you can hardly wait to see opened for the joy you hope it will bring; there are those long-cherished, familiar faces, soon to be reunited around a tree, a table, a glowing fireside; there are those quiet, even holy moments up ahead, when time stands still, and suddenly becomes filled beyond all containing. Anticipation—looking forward for Christmas—is a major, perhaps even the very best part of this holy season.

Searching among my own earliest memories I find that many of them share this same tantalizing feeling. Counting down the days, hours, and finally, at long last, minutes, until the dismissal bell rang for the last time, school was over for a week at least, and—splendid before me—lay the Christmas holidays, rich with promise, overflowing with potential delight. Or lying in bed, head swimming with possibilities, calculating the strategic moment, that not too outrageously early predawn hour when it might be permissible to steal downstairs and view the array of wonders heaped beneath the tree.

Anticipation is a most uniquely human experience, something, strange as it may seem, that we tend to treasure and recall long after we have forgotten whatever it was we were actually looking forward to. In fact it is my own persuasion that this anticipation, this "having something to look forward to," is not only a feature of this one particular season, but a vital ingredient in all of our living, in every season of the year.

Viktor Frankl, in his far-reaching book, *Man's Search for Meaning*, emphasizes how vitally, at times even devastatingly important this was to his fellow prisoners in Auschwitz concentration camp. He describes a friend, a formerly well-known composer, who told Frankl of a dream, a dream that they would all be liberated on March 30, 1945. As that date drew near with no news of release his friend's health slipped into decline. On March 29 he developed a raging fever. On March 30 he lost consciousness. On the 31st he died. "To all outward appearances," Frankl writes, "he died of typhus." But he really died from having nothing left to look forward to. He died of crushed anticipation.

So it is, on a lesser scale, with us: that trip, that vacation up ahead, that next promotion, job offer, check in the mail, the new whatever-it-is that the savings account is inching toward, that evening out, that telephone call, that visit, break in the routine; we all need something to look forward to. It is what makes the rest of our humdrum days endurable. We live toward, we live for, we live by our anticipations.

This tendency, however, while universal, is not invariably beneficial. The long, sad record of human disappointment is filled with those who spent years, even lifetimes, preparing for some crowning event—a marriage, the return of a lover, the birth of a child, the call to duty or high office—something long expected that never came about. Again, how many there are who have looked forward to something so intensely—graduation, release from the service, a new position, retirement—that the present, the actual daily living of life faded to insignificance and became dead time, empty time, time only to be endured until the great day, whatever it was, arrived. We talk nowadays of "killing time," yet do not seem to realize that such killing constitutes not murder, but suicide. We do need something to look forward to, but we cannot permit anticipation to nullify the life we hold in our hands here and now.

There is a deeper level involved here—if we dare—an even more difficult and testing question that must be faced. Is not all anticipation finally doomed, an exercise in ultimate futility? That ruthlessly honest intellect Samuel Johnson wrote:

> It is necessary to hope, though hope should aways be deluded: for hope itself is happiness and its frustrations, however frequent, are yet less dreadful than its extinction.[2]

We need hope. As human animals we must have something to look toward. But, in the last analysis, is this not simply a game we play, a pleasant, relatively harmless way to ease the inescapable passage of the years? Is not all our anticipation condemned to inevitable failure in this wintered world where, at the close, we all face death alone? As Shakespeare expresses it so elegaically in *Cymbeline*:

> Golden lads and lasses all must,
> As chimney sweepers come to dust (Act 4, Scene 2).

So we come to the age-old question of Advent which, for all the festive trappings of this season, finds its echo, if we will hear it, within each one of us. *Watchman tell us of the night*, what, if any, are its signs of hope, its portents of promise? Is there an anticipation which is *not* inevitably doomed? Is there, can there ever be, something to look forward to that will not disappoint, that will actually justify the years of longing, will live up to, even exceed, our wildest dreams? Is there honestly any hope, any word from any Lord, any enduring vision to pass on to our children, any prospect that can truly bear fulfilment in this world of relentless aging, and of raging epidemic, of terror, famine, and resurgent, inhuman violence, of loneliness never fully comforted, of the utter drear finality of death?

So comes Advent. Not the Santa Claus commercial come-on, but the steady, irresistible preparation of the ages for blossoming, for fulfilment. So comes Advent, takes all the false and failed

2. Johnson, "No. 58.," n.p.

anticipations of our days, the good dreams and the bad, dashed hopes, lost longings never fulfilled, and tells us, "Yes," and tells us, "Pray," and tells us,

And what I say to you I say to all: "Watch."

All those intimations, those vague, undefined moments glimpsed, then vanished before ever fully formed, let alone defined, those yearnings that surprise in the middle of a symphony, at the close of a novel, before a star-lit summer night or frost-touched winter dawn, that strange yet certain sense of standing on the threshold, poised on the edge of something, and that something is something beautiful, ineffably peaceful, inexpressibly good; to all of these comes Advent, and tells us, "Yes," and sets our feet on the road toward Christmas, advising us, " . . . what I say to you I say to all: "Watch."

What the specifics will be, the guest list, menu, order of the speeches, toasts and dances, all this we cannot know, at least not yet. This much we *can* say, however, for it has been given to us of old: whatever our anticipation, when it comes it will have something to do with birth, with a new world entered, a new family discovered, a new way of seeing light and dark, of touching, tasting, knowing, being.

Again, it will surely have to do with the giving and receiving of gifts, this whatever-it-is we anticipate: giving openly, honestly, and with all our hearts, and receiving in the same way, which can be much more complicated for independent, individual souls such as we are.

It will demand much in terms of priorities, this future of ours when it arrives, leaving behind flocks, kingdoms, inns, all manner of other busy doings, in order to kneel, and to behold, to be healed, and then simply to be.

It will be all caught up with love, this anticipation of ours when realized, the passionate love of a lover, the strong, self-giving love of a mother, the tender, protective love of a father, the trusting, innocent, deep-demanding love of a child, that asks of you only your life, and then gives it back, renewed, within the simplest, most innocent of smiles.

It will have everything to do with a newborn child, whatever it is we can look forward to; and that means it will be most natural, most gentle, soft, vulnerable, yet with an immense, world-embracing power to evoke the good from people, to call forth the truth, to bring about blessing, to reconcile, call together and unite, to build the foundations of peace.

Something to look forward to then, something about a birth, a baby, a gift, a greeting, a God who gives, and lives, and loves to the very end, and then beyond. This is the true anticipation of Advent. This is the goal of all our aspiration, expectation. And for this, this Advent morning, we are warned to "Watch," to "Look out," to "Get ready," to live each day in the power of this promise, the promise of our gracious God made present in our midst, and for our blessing, until he comes again.

∼

Prepare me for the simple wonder of your coming, Lord Christ.
And let my life show forth your present risen power, the promise of
your kingdom, the glory of your grace. Amen.

Friday

Advent's Secret

The

wonder

of it rests

within the waiting

all the ways that our

impatience can be tempered

slowly weaned from the demands

of the immediate, taught to savor

moments, cherish every living

instant as it passes, not

only for itself but for

the promise that it

bears of life

to come.

ADVENT'S REMINDER

This season makes quotidian reality more real,
marking with ceremony the passing of each day,
as if we sought to hasten the relentless dwindling
of the hours until there are no more.

Expectation is the key,
what it is that we believe awaits us there,
where time, and everything we know runs out.

Will there be a judgment scene
when record books are balanced, debts repaid,
a time for retribution and reward?

Is there nothing there at all,
complete oblivion, without even
the perception of non-being?

Or must we, may we, tread this time-bound way
toward Bethlehem—held tight somewhere between
desire and dread—yet still seeing that this very day
may be the best we have for living in?

Cataloguing

They proliferate this time of year,
cram tight into the mailbox, to come leaping out
when you turn the key, like spawning salmon surging
past the dam. A glossy, multi-colored cornucopia they seem,
overflowing with desirables, collectibles, adorables: books,
bicycles, and bonnets, toys, ties, trees and trimmings too,
all those items that you never knew you absolutely needed
to make these holy days complete.
An array, indeed, a hoard of gleaming idols
that would make old Aaron's golden calf look tawdry
in comparison. Take two tablets, so advised the wise man
on the mountain, and check back in the morning.
On that morning when, with all the wrappings opened,
you look around and realize the gift lies in the giving,
the receiving too, and all the glitter and the gold—
forget the price—is left there, long forgotten,
among the trampled straw beneath the manger.

STALL FOR CHRISTMAS

No room! No room! The age-old cry of Bethlehem
rings clear across these centuries tonight, while we
wait, engine idling, prepared to pounce the moment
some newly successful celebrant gets here to drive

one

car

off

clear one space for fresh, aspiring pilgrims, such as
we, who seek, not place to rest our weary heads, or
lay a newborn baby, but deliverance to go and buy
our heart's desire with plastic money, borrowed time.

Saturday

GIFTS OF ADVENT II
Patience

If it seem slow, wait for it; it will surely come, it will not delay.

—HABAKKUK 2:3

For the creation waits with eager longing for the revealing of the children of God.

—ROMANS 8:19

Lessons, revelations, redefinitions of reality, were all part of everyday experience during my years of ministry in New York City. One busy day during the holiday season I stumbled upon the New York definition of eternity. I was loading packages onto the elevator at our apartment building and the person already in there was urging me to slow down. "No need to rush," she assured me. "This elevator is so slow it's like eternity." "In fact," she added, "I timed it once. I said to myself, 'This thing takes an eternity so I'll time it.' Forty-five seconds . . . *forty-five seconds* from the twelfth floor to the lobby." There you have it. In New York City eternity takes forty-five seconds.

On another occasion, driving back into the city late on the Friday after Thanksgiving, I found myself backed up among the chaotic traffic lines at the Holland Tunnel and checking lanes on either side to see if they might be moving a fraction faster, so that, by judicious switching and obnoxious driving, I might save forty, maybe even fifty seconds. And all this so that I could get home in time to write my Sunday sermon on the theme of "Patience." It was then that I realized—not for the first time—that my sermons tend to be addressed—these meditations, too—primarily to myself. On the other hand, I do suspect that many who read these words on patience need to heed them almost as much as I do.

Yet another remembered scene from New York days has me standing in a skyscraper-encircled courtyard watching three Tibetan monks painstakingly crafting, out of colored sand, an intricate peace mandala. The scene constituted a powerful call to quietness, meditation, prayer. And the people who stood around watching took two whole minutes, some of them even three, before glancing at their watches and hurrying away. I, being of a more spiritual orientation, actually lingered for close to five minutes; but I was probably memorizing the scene for a poem or sermon illustration. "Lord, grant me patience," goes that typical prayer of our hyperactive world,

> Grant me, O God, the gift of patience . . . and do please
> hurry it up!

One might ask, who needs patience anyway? Maybe in those antiquated days fifty years or so ago, patience might have been a virtue; but in an age of smartphones, Twitter and Facebook, of 3-D printers, laser scanners, zero-to-sixty in five seconds, and instant everything, who needs it? When time is money, and the fast lane is the only place to be, this patience thing, this willingness to wait around, only makes you a prime candidate to fall behind, to lose your place, to fail.

On the other hand, for all our amazing/alarming technology, all our ability to move information and money faster than a speeding bullet, we still do an awful lot of waiting. Waiting for an airplane, or a subway train, a green light, an elevator, a check to clear, a sales clerk to look up, or just holding, still holding on the telephone. There is that anxious waiting for test results, academic tests, hospital tests. Waiting for a child to grow up and become independent. Waiting for a wound to heal, a word of forgiveness, or remorse to be spoken, a basic gesture of affection and tenderness. Despite our instant society, our addiction to immediate gratification, satisfaction on demand, we still do a whole lot of waiting.

So we turn back in this Advent season to these Scriptures that have nourished and guided us across the centuries, and there we find text after text about waiting, about patience. Thus the Psalmist of old:

> I believe that I shall see the goodness of the Lord in the land of the living! Wait for the Lord, be strong, and let your heart take courage; yea, wait for the Lord! (Ps 27:13–14).

And Isaiah, in immortal words:

> They that wait upon the Lord shall renew their strength; they shall mount up with wings as eagles; they shall run, and not be weary; and they shall walk, and not faint. (Isa 40:31).

The very best things in life—despite our hurry-up offenses and rapid response teams, our lightning this and instant that—so many of the things we seek after and cherish simply have to be waited for; they require, demand our patience. They have their own clocks, their own timetable, and we have to let them take the time they need, *all* the time they need.

We've seen a lot, over these recent decades, of what one might call instant relationships, that kind of passionate loving in which nothing is held back, nothing delayed, every single thing has to be experienced here and now. We have also seen a vast and tragic toll in broken homes, battered spouses, lost and abused children, sexually transmitted disease, the shredding of the fabric of society. Surely this is telling us that love too, love above all else, demands time, requires patience, must have that unique kind of long-term, through-thick-and-thin commitment, if it is ever to become again the blessing God entrusted to our care so long ago.

God too demands our patience. His clock is not ours. His time cannot be shaped, adjusted to our schedules. Might that be why we see so little of the genuine experience of God, the presence of the Divine in our days? We are in too much of a hurry. In this age of immediate gratification we attempt to pray; and finding what we perceive to be no one at home, we hang up. Never for us the experience of saints of old who knew at times, just as we do, the arid desert, the icy winter of the soul, the bleak sense of God's absence. Yet they persevered in prayer until emptiness was filled, until their weakness became sufficient for God's strength to be displayed. As Maria Boulding, a contemplative nun from England, has put it:

> God brings us to these winters, these dreary times of deadness and emptiness of spirit, as truly as he brings winter after autumn, as a necessary step towards next spring . . . Our strength can sometimes be a greater obstacle to God's work than our weakness . . . When our ego is humbled and not obstructing, God's creative Spirit can often have freer play. Like the bare trees, it may be that we allow the glory to shine through at these times more purely than in our summer prosperity.[3]

It seems to me there are two kinds of patience, two basic varieties of expectation. I heard a scientist from MIT speak about, of all things, the second coming of our Lord. He used two fascinating analogies to speak about delay in expectation. "Suppose," he told us, "that an unexploded bomb, fallen on London during World War II, was lying there still, buried beneath the rubble." The longer the delay, he pointed out, the more likely it would be that the bomb would not explode, that its death-dealing mechanism had gone awry. But now suppose we have an alarm clock, fully wound, and set to go off at some random time within the next twelve hours. The longer the delay, in this case, the more likely it is that the alarm will sound in the next hour, the next ten minutes, the next ten seconds. There are two kinds of waiting, two kinds of patience.

3. Boulding, *The Coming of God*, 91.

This patience the Scriptures lay upon us, this waiting that we know during these expectant weeks of Advent, is no grim, tight-lipped test of our endurance, no passive gutting-it-out to the bitter end. The patience of the believer, the endurance that the New Testament calls for, even in face of suffering and tribulation, is a patience that is filled with hope, and accompanied by joy. It is a patience grounded deep in faith, faith that things are moving steadily, however slowly it may seem, toward a goal, a goal of glory, faith that the night, even the darkest of nights, is turning toward an inevitable sunrise. So Paul can write:

> I consider that the sufferings of this present time are not worth comparing with the glory that is to be revealed to us. For the creation waits with eager longing for the revealing of the children of God (Rom 8:18–19).

Here is the patience to which we are called in this season. No weary, drawn-out, seemingly unending winter vigil; but an eager expectation of the coming of the Lord, of the birth within our hearts of the Son of God, our Savior.

So let us accept God's gift of patience for this Advent. Let us take time, in these weeks so pressed for time, take time to wait, and hope, to listen, and to wonder. We can schedule all we want in this highly scheduled season—Christmas shopping, Christmas mailing, Christmas concerts, Christmas parties—but only God can choose the time for his coming into our midst. And without that, all the rest is busy work.

Take time then, these few weeks, to watch the winter light, those glorious December sunsets. Take time to listen for the winter birds, those brave companions who linger with us through the frigid months, or for music, which speaks to us in ways that can both fascinate the mind and move the heart. Take time to play with children, and with friends, and rediscover the sheer joy of aimless relaxation. Take time to craft a simple gift with love and tender care, or write a note to friends far away. Take time and patience to find God, or rather to let God find you. He will not force his way through all the clutter and confusion of our days. But if we open up a door, a quiet moment, in the church, by the tree, with the book, and then wait with genuine patience, this is the season when the holy child can be born into our hearts.

≈

Lord, grant me the gift of patience. Then bless my waiting with a foretaste of your glory, with the living presence of your Son, our Lord. Amen.

Advent Week Three

Sunday

SOMETHING FOR CHRISTMAS III
Something Worth Praying For

For a child has been born for us, a son given to us; authority rests upon his shoulders; and he is named, Wonderful Counselor, Mighty God, Everlasting Father, Prince of Peace.

—ISAIAH 9:6

This Advent season, in church tradition, is not only a time of expectancy and waiting, not just a time of looking forward and hoping; it is also a time for praying. Indeed, along with Lent, Advent has long been observed as a period when Christians have intensified their devotional life, have reclaimed the disciplines of prayer, have sought to renew neglected spiritual resources. Visit any religious bookstore over these December weeks and the sheer volume and weight of publications in the area of prayer and meditation—"Spirituality," as they call it—can drive you to your knees, if nothing else will.

Yet, while Lent, those lengthening days of late winter/early spring, does naturally lend itself to such pursuits, I must confess that these Advent days, these last few weeks before Christmas present much more of a challenge. In fact it is my suspicion that, for many, the only prayers to be uttered amid the holiday rush and hustle are what I call, *Good God Prayers*: "*Good God*, is it that late already?" "*Good God*, what are all these people doing in the post office at eight in the morning?" "*Good God*, what happened to Christmas, anyway? Where did it go?"

On the other hand, there *are* those letters to Santa Claus; and if anything nowadays can be said to come close to actual prayer, perhaps they fit the bill. I am reminded of the youngster in a popular cartoon who is depicted, leaning on a punctured pigskin, musing to himself:

> I need a new football. I don't know if I should send up
> a prayer, write a letter to Santa Claus, or call Grandma.

That's the trouble, of course, with so many of our prayers; they tend to be solely concerned with things and how to obtain them, or with escapes, ways out of impossible situations. There's a lively old story about this in which someone asks God, "How long is a thousand years to you?" To which the Eternal One replies, "Oh, just one second." "Well then, Almighty, how much is a million dollars to you?" The Creator shrugs it off as, "No more than a penny." With a gleam in his eye, and a smile creeping across his face, the inquisitor poses one last question, "Lord, can I have just one penny?" To which Omniscience responds, "Perhaps, but in just one second."

What then *is* worth praying for? What might there be, beyond the Christmas lists and the latest global crisis, that could bring us to our knees in honest prayer, even in this busiest, most packed and panicked season? There is, of course, our concern for others. Each Sabbath day, and every *single* day in many places, in sanctuaries of all varieties across this land, people bow their heads to pray, not chiefly for themselves, but for family and friends, for this world and its wretched ones, for those who face illness, bereavement, turmoil. And all that is certainly something worth praying for.

But what about ourselves? Is there something about our own selves that is worthy of our prayers, worth spending time on our knees, searching the scriptures, gazing within, and without, and above? Do we ourselves have anything worth praying for? The answer here can be different for each one who reads these words.

For some—ironically enough—it is a moment of peace *from* others that they pray for, a brief surcease from all the pressures, demands, responsibilities, of daily, hourly love. For others the need is for someone *to* love, someone to feel responsible for, to care deeply about, to share their daily joys and pains. For some it might be a job, a steady income, the assurance of security and self-worth; others, again, seek freedom to let go, take time off, become that fuller person who has been swallowed up within the all-enveloping identity of what he or she does for a living. For some, perhaps, the need is for the healing of an ancient, festering wound or grudge; others may seek deliverance from a very present fear. Something worth praying for.

Then what is it that we get? When all the prayers, candle lighting, carol singing has finally run its course, what is it that we receive for all this effort? Isaiah made that clear long ago:

> For to us a child is born, to us a son is given . . . (Isa 9:6).

Or, as Luke's angel told those startled shepherds:

> For to you is born this day in the city of David a Savior, who is Christ the Lord. And this will be a sign for you: you will find a babe . . . (Luke 2:11–12).

A child, then, a newborn infant, that is God's answer to our prayers, to all those needs and wishes, those fears and dreams we thought of just a moment ago, to the prayers of all the centuries since first we humankind lifted hands and voices toward the heavens.

I've been watching children, little children, recently; catching sight of them in those marvelous carrying pods parents pop them into at the post office, toy store, potluck supper and the like; they're to be found these days all over the place, once you start to pay attention. I've been noticing again the inner peacefulness of infants. Oh yes, I fully realize that children have been known to fuss from time to time. After four children of our own and three grandchildren I will not soon forget that indisputable reality. But, when they are *not* fussing there is about them that sense of inner calm and trust, a confidence these fortunate youngsters have—that each and every child deserves to have, must have, if our society is ever to become truly human. This is a confidence that all is basically well, that they are cherished, cared for, held and watched over by strong, protective arms.

There is that bewitchingly wondering gaze these little ones can turn upon a parent, their own fingers, the living room carpet, or a total stranger. There is the way they have of casting spells on all our adult soberness so that we become, like them, just a bit silly, find ourselves making curious noises, funny faces, tender, touching gestures, things we had not realized were still inside us waiting to be called forth, set free once more. Give them half a chance, these little ones, and they will take advantage of you, will slip a blessing in beneath your guard and leave you strangely humbled, enlivened, maybe even just a bit reborn. "For unto you is born . . . a child . . . a Savior."

I walked into a hospital room, stood beside a sickbed, and there lay an old friend and partner in ministry over many years. My colleague had suffered a cerebral hemorrhage and was deep in a coma, not expected to recover. Yet the thing that struck me right away was this: how young, how peaceful, how at rest he looked. In an odd way he was just like those little children, only at the other end, the opposite extreme of life, back again on the doorstep of eternity. There was that same uncanny sense of trust, that all is in good hands, the very best of hands, that the truly vital things, of hope, joy, of benediction, are fully taken care of, that, at the end as in the beginning, all is, all will be, well.

Something worth praying for then, the gift of a child to save us, that "blessed assurance" we often sing about, that eternal trust that, in the manger child, God names us, each one, as his children and claims us, now and forever, for his own.

Let go, and let God; that's what prayer can be for you and me in this time of rushing to and fro, a liberated moment to relax, to re-create, to realize we are just where we belong, we are where we have always been, and to entrust ourselves into the hands that shaped this world, those pierced hands that bore our sins upon the tree, those guiding hands that shape our lives this very day and fit them for eternity.

~

Answer our prayers, dear Lord, with the simple gift of trust, the blessing of true faith, the steady, calm, assurance that your love, in Christ, is for us, and forever. Amen.

Monday

An Advent Prayer

In this season of hectic preparation, Lord, we find ourselves beset by a sense of being perpetually unready. There is so much to do, so many tasks to be scheduled, undertaken, and completed. There are cards to be bought, written, and mailed, gifts to be planned and purchased, trees to be trimmed, secrets to be concealed, parties to be planned, concerts, plays, visits, to be arranged, provisions, food and drink, to be laid in for this entire festive season. So much, Lord, so many things to be prepared for.

We find ourselves not ready. For, no matter how we plan, no matter how far in advance we begin, there always seems to come a time when things fall apart, someone gets sick, the weather intervenes, the schedule comes unglued, and we begin to wonder if we will ever make it. Lord, what breathless, bustling, busy times these are! Times in which we feel that, despite all efforts, we are still not ready, not ready for Christmas.

And yet you come to us just the same, right at the heart of our unreadiness, just as you did on that first Christmas long ago. You catch us unawares, with a carol on the radio in morning traffic, in the heat of a messy, cluttered, kitchen, halfway through a stack of envelopes and cards, in the eyes of a child as her face is washed for church. You speak to us and say, "Relax now. Take a moment. Know peace. My Son is now yours, after all, my Christmas gift for all the ages. So cherish him amid the bustle. Never forget just why he came, why he still comes. And give yourself to him, that you might share the joy of being born anew in this most tender season." Lord, we are grateful that you do still come, even in the midst of our unreadiness, you still come to share with us the gift of your promise, the blessing of your peace. Amen.

MID ADVENT

John the Baptist Sunday looms,
its caustic, antiseptic word, slicing
surgically clean through all those wistful songs,
the peering after dim and distant stars.

Meanwhile expectancy is beginning
to wear thin, considering the many times
we've been through this before. There appears
to be a slowdown in the countdown
and distraction heaped on weariness makes
the raising, even of the head, a major undertaking,
the girding of the loins, far too much
even to contemplate.

Right here—at the half-way point—
is where Christmas is decided.
Will it stagger on toward its usual,
bottom-line return? Or might there be
an ambush up ahead, where we will meet,
be met by, one who's urgent call to turn around
caused kings and priests to tremble?
Hold on tight!

ADVENT SATURDAY

(With Catriona in New York)

Hanging on beside you as the crosstown bus
lurches its laden way between the wintered hills
of Central Park, my sidelong glance snags
on a prospect never caught before,
glimpsing within your early teenage profile
the full maturity of middle age,
the aspect you may wear one day as mother,
matron, one who bears the future on firm shoulders.

    But see now what the eyes betray
    in that slightest hint of drawing down toward
    the edge, as though a weariness lies buried there,
    waiting to be born.
    My own well-worn, paternal eyes
    seek momentary refuge.
    Only to be captured, upon opening,
    by the clear, unclouded sunrise of your smile.

Thanking the Great Provider of such moments
over thirteen years of grace, I leave the crowded bus,
lead you dashing across Madison, into elegant Saint James'
to meet, beneath the Advent wreath, a harpsichord
and string ensemble, rehearsing with the soloists
tomorrow's version of Messiah.

> *Behold a virgin shall conceive,*
> *And bear a son,*
> *And shall call his name,*
> *Immanuel—God with us.*

And through a sudden storm of tears
I grasp the wounding, mending, holly branch,
claiming the spiral mystery of word-made-flesh
and secret lodged within the solemn
turning of the years.

LATE CALL

What do the geese cry
   one to another, angling
      across the early winter sky
         this Advent morning? Surely
            it is a call of courage, of sheer
               encouragement passing by, the
                  cheering hope, keen expectation
                    of neglectful fields, smooth waters
                       up ahead before the darkness settles in.
                    Today I waited for them knowing high
                  within the bones—far from my brain
                but somehow surer—they would wing
              along and lift and carry me to spy
            this bright, full world that waits
          beyond the vee, prepares to greet
        our landing, honking, jostling
shrill arrival. Oh, take me!

Tuesday

How Many Miles to Bethlehem? III

The Journey

Then Jacob awoke from sleep and said, "Surely the Lord is in this place; and I did not know it." And he was afraid and said, "How awesome is this place! This is none other than the house of God, and this is the gate of heaven."

—GENESIS 28:16–17

Therefore do not be anxious about tomorrow, for tomorrow will be anxious for itself. Let the day's own trouble be sufficient for the day.

—MATTHEW 6:34

It is not at all surprising that the Son of God, Jesus the Christ, was born in the midst of a journey, arrived on the scene in a time of hurrying to and fro and homelessness, found his first resting place in a rough and makeshift shelter. This entire Bible is filled with journeys, crisscrossed with travel narratives, loaded with stories recounted on the run. From Adam and Eve cast out from Eden, through Abraham setting forth in faith, Jacob fleeing his angry brother Esau, Joseph and his sojourn down in Egypt, Moses' forty years of wandering in the wilderness, Joshua's triumphal progress through the Promised Land, then later the sad transit into Babylonian exile, and the glorious return sung of by Isaiah, all the way to Jesus' journeys around ancient Palestine, and Paul's missionary voyages, these Scriptures can be seen, in many ways, as a travel book. They tell how a people on the move, a wandering, nomadic people—not all that unlike ourselves—are joined in their journeying, are encountered, wrestled with, and transformed by, the God who summoned them to venture forth in the first place.

And it is not only the Bible that displays this fascination with the open road. Throughout the vast library of literature from *Gilgamesh* and *The Odyssey*, through Chaucer's *Canterbury Tales*, Bunyan's *Pilgrim's Progress*, on to the latest installment of *Star Wars*, from the morning walk around *Walden Pond*, to the furthest reaches of the universe, we humankind have described our days, viewed our lives, explored our souls, within the context of a journey, a setting-out, a steady progression despite setbacks and diversions, toward a final welcoming, the ultimate attainment of the goal.

The problem, at least for me and, I suspect, for many others in our time, is that no sooner do I think about a journey than I feel the need to rush ahead, to ask questions about where we are going, how long it will take to get there—"Are we there yet, Daddy?"— and what we will find when we arrive. I become impatient with the day-to-day stuff, that slow-but-steady progression that must take place, and find myself just wanting to get through with it and on to whatever it is comes next. In other words, I find it much more easy to look *ahead* than to look *around*, to anticipate rather than to contemplate.

Back in my youth in Scotland, in those days before everyone owned a car, we would hire a bus and go off on day trips together; our church youth fellowship used to do this. One favorite excursion would be called "The Mystery Trip," when we would board the bus without the faintest idea of where we were bound. What fun we had as we watched for every intersection, every signpost, every fork in the road, trying to project just where we were going to end up. There were times when I wasn't sure even the bus driver knew for certain. I suspect he headed for those rare spots where, in our ever-damp Scottish climate, it might not be actually raining at that present moment. One thing about those "Mystery Trips" however: they made us pay attention; they taught us to keep a keen eye on the road.

We lose so much—I do at least—when all I'm doing is focusing up ahead, anticipating getting there already, planning the details of arrival and settling in, and barely tolerating the time in between, wishing it away so that the goal may be attained, the destination gained all the sooner. Thus the journey becomes something to be gotten over with as swiftly as possible, empty time, lost time, an unfortunate obstacle between you and the next thing and then the next.

I have a hunch that Jacob felt something like that. He had just cheated his twin brother—his aged father too—out of the family inheritance; and that brother was a rough-and-ready, hunting-fishing, outdoorsman with a fierce, redheaded temper. Better to get moving, better to clear out till things cool off. So there Jacob was, on the run, bedding down in the wilderness with a cold, hard rock for his pillow. As he fell asleep, it's my bet that his mind was busy with plans, weighing destinations, potential refuges, places where he might settle down a while, find a wife, raise some kids, flocks as well, build up an inheritance of his own so that he wouldn't be so vulnerable to his brother's rage. Then came that dream—a ladder up to heaven, God's angels moving up and down.

> Then Jacob awoke from his sleep and said, "Surely the Lord is in this place; and I did not know it." And he was afraid and said, "How awesome is this place! This is none other than the house of God, and this is the gate of heaven."

In Jacob's desperate rush to get away, to move on to the next phase, he was brought up short, stopped dead, or rather *alive*, in his tracks by the vision of God, God's presence, God's reality all about him.

Years later, fourteen years—seven for Leah, seven for Rachel—Jacob is on his way back home with his wives, his children, his now enormous wealth in flocks and herds. Once again he spends a night alone in the wilderness. And once again his mind must have been racing ahead, to the meeting on the morrow with his brother, to how Esau might respond to the gifts—peace offerings—he had sent on ahead, and to his wives and children waiting on the farther side of the brook. Then comes this strange encounter, this wrestling with the spirit until dawn, a struggle through which Jacob finds himself transformed, renamed as *Israel*, and sent forth, limping, over the horizon of a new and splendid sunrise.

We gobble down our days for the most part. We race along from one hour, week, month, to the next, and suddenly it's Advent again, and there's even more to be got through if we're ever going to make it to Christmas and all that Christmas means. But listen for a moment. Can you hear the voice of Jacob? Can you catch, across the centuries, a word that calls you to slow down, look around, dream just a bit, then pay attention to what that dream is saying. Realize that this now is all you've got. The future . . . who knows? The past . . . beyond recall. The journey, this very journey you are on right now, has a meaning all its own, a meaning that begins when you awake, wherever you are, and say:

> How awesome is this place! This is none other than the house of God, and this the gate of heaven.

What was it that carpenter from Nazareth told us?

> Don't go worrying about tomorrow. Tomorrow can worry about itself (Matt 6:34).

"One day at a time," that's what they live by, swear by, in Alcoholics Anonymous. "One . . . day . . . at . . . a . . . time." Sometimes I ask myself if we are all recovering addicts, time-aholics, hooked tight into this race toward the future, never daring to pull up short, to pause and look around. And what we need to do is dream a little, wrestle with whatever our demons may be, until they bless us, renew us, rename us, send us forth to life, one blessed day at a time.

One of my own favorite Advent traditions is to attend, even at times to sing along at a performance of Handel's *Messiah*. Not too long ago I was sitting at such an event, perched in the very back row, since I was to present an Advent poetry program of my own in a nearby church later that same evening. Thinking ahead, preoccupied, planning for a speedy getaway, I was surprised, caught up and carried away by the splendor of the long familiar music. "Why

. . ." it dawned on me, "why, these are all dances. These are lively, stately dances Handel is offering to us here!" You see, no matter the solemnity of the words, no matter the weighty biblical text being sung, my rebellious foot would not stop tapping. The simple explanation, the musicological explanation, is that Handel composed *The Messiah* weaving in many of the melodies and compositions he had written earlier for secular occasions. But there was more to it than that. The dance that is *Messiah*, if you will only hear it, stops you in your tracks, arrests that insane, headlong rush toward whatever—God knows what—and sets your feet to moving, sets your toes to tapping, sets your mind to dreaming about angels, sets your soul to struggling to be reborn. Handel was right; if we're going to journey toward the Messiah then we'd better be ready for the dance.

In one of the best pieces of advice she ever received, a church worker colleague was told by her elderly mother:

Joan, never throw away your dancing shoes.

Because it's never too late for the Lord of the dance.

So there it is, the journey. No mere empty transition from one place into another. Not just the vacant interval between departure and arrival. Life itself, every blessed moment of it. The present, this very here and now, God's Christmas present gift wrapped for you to open and rejoice in. Don't miss it. Please don't miss it. For if you do, when you actually get there, wherever your *there* may be, there may be nothing in the place, nobody there to greet you.

> Then Jacob awoke from his sleep and said, "Surely the Lord is in this place; and I did not know it." And he was afraid and said, "How awesome is this place! This is none other than the house of God, and this is the gate of heaven."

~

Lord, send a star to guide us, that on our darkened path your light might lead us onward, step by daily step, toward the manger, the mystery, the miracle. Amen.

Wednesday

Seasonal Decor

We bring them out again,
these relics of a score of Advents Past,
unwind with reverent gentleness
the yellowed tissue bindings,
and remember where they hail from,
how they first became a feature of
our annual time of expectation,
conjuring again the market place in Prague,
that old cathedral shop—long gone—in Chartres,
and the frigid night the doctor came to call,
bursting through the door to bring, not pills,
thermometer, or needles, but that tall, rich-carved,
and triple-tiered, Christmas-candle-powered windmill
with its circling scenes of shepherds, angels,
journeying magi, and the starlit manger.
He never paused to tell of how its fragile flame
had lit the final Advent bedside of his wife
of thirty years and more, simply said that
our four girls might enjoy something like this
to watch beside and wait for Christmas Eve.
All kinds of things, this time of year,
can wear the secret sheen of sacredness.
Might it be the word made flesh was born
to say precisely that?

AFTERSHAVE

Try a little Eternity, he murmured,
gently spritzing me, as I powered through
the *Miracle on 34th Street* doors of Macy's,
intent on finding one last thing
to make my Christmas list complete.
Try a little Eternity.

And stopped me short, mid headlong dash,
to say, Why not? A splash of aftershave—
Quelle est cette odeur agréable?—
might even bring a fragment (figment?)
of that frankincensing cowshed, to bless
my frantic quest with momentary mystery,
a rare fragrance sorely wanting
in this flagrant race to beat the twenty-fifth.

Who knows but, at that higher,
heavenlier, turnstile, the old geezer
perched behind The Book might just lean
across his podium with a celestial spray-gun
of his own and, spritzing madly, murmur,
Here Barrie, now try a little Eternity.

TRIMMING

We
did
the tree
again tonight
—family style—
with all the usual,
traditional disputes
about which box to open
first, who gets to hang what,
precisely where to set the Shains'
glass bird which has survived (Praise God!)
seven such arguments already.
The lower branches were,
as is the custom, heavy-laden,
three or four gems per stem, while only
a few furtive adult transfers rescued the
last two feet from stark and lonely nudity.
The lights flickered for a moment
and went out, necessitating testing
each and every tiny oriental bulb
(or were they Italian?)
at least three times. The flasher either
didn't work or worked too well, till somehow
it relented and the show was on.
Turn
out
the
light,
a truce to every running
fight, come see what is
reflected for one instant
in tomorrow's wide
dark eyes.

ORANGE ALERT

(December 2002)

This new-awakened terror
that marks and stalks our days,
defines the news, and redirects all journeys,
will withstand, of course, our efforts to ignore,
deny, divert its shadow to those other folk,
those more productive targets.

Even in these customary days of festival
and feasting, its insistent presence spills across
and stains our ceremonies with a sudden apprehension.
Images of flame and falling, dust and utter darkness,
captivity and stark, remorseless violence, invade
and violate the sanctum, replacing memory
and hope with glimpses of an unfamiliar fear,
prompting us to look again with care toward
the ones who walk, have walked, beside us.

But then, this holy season—
fraught with news of Caesars, cattle-sheds and swords,
the blood of innocents and sudden, urgent flight—
has ever sought, beneath the layers
of sentiment and song, to teach us this:
a dark and threatening world,
a mother, father, child,
a respite from the storm, however brief,
and what is to be feared,
and what is not.

Thursday

Looking for Christmas III
Look Up For Christmas

Now when these things begin to take place, look up and raise your heads, because your redemption is drawing near.

—LUKE 21:28

If there is one essential ingredient apparently missing from these early twenty-first-century Christmases it is surely the presence of angels. Try as you will to reassemble that classic Christmas Eve scenario: shepherds we could manage, there are still a few about, though they have probably been declared redundant. ("Technological obsolescence" is how their fate would be described today.) The same, I suspect, holds true for stables, mangers, and sheep. The stars still move across the heavens as they have always done. There are even a few kings left, although, apart from those persistent British royals, it's getting harder and harder to make up a quorum of three. But as for angels—we seem to be experiencing a definite dearth of angels.

It certainly was not ever thus. Look, for example, at that first Christmas, where we seem to come across one heavenly being after another, with angels appearing to Zechariah and Elizabeth, to Joseph and Mary, to the wise men, and then that entire celestial chorale of angels, associate angels, assistant angels, all vocalizing for the benefit of those astonished Bethlehem shepherds. To anyone "looking up for Christmas" back then the sky must have seemed crammed to capacity, a veritable Times Square of heavenly beings speeding to and fro like so many frantic shoppers, seeking to get everything accomplished within "the fullness of time."

Looking up for Christmas these days, however, the only angelic hosts *we* are likely to observe will be of the tinfoil or styrofoam variety. Their golden plastic trumpets will sound, not the harmonies of heaven, but somewhat more mundane melodies:

> Angels we have heard on high
> telling us go out and buy.
>
> Hark, the herald angels sing,
> you can charge most everything.

There is no escaping the fact that we are living today in a time of the apparent absence of angels.

Where, then, did they go? What on earth, or in heaven, happened to Luke's "multitude of the heavenly host"? Several possible avenues toward explanation come to mind. For one: if this holiday season turns out to be anything like recent ones, we might suppose that those angels, like the transportation workers, teachers, sanitation people, and police, are out on strike and, pending binding arbitration, may even yet make it back by early next week. An alternative approach, especially for those who have viewed the recent spate of horror movies, is to suppose that these supernatural beings have all had better job offers from Hollywood and are currently masquerading on screen as demons, devils, zombies and the like.

But the real reason, it seems to me, behind this regrettable absence is that we no longer believe we inhabit that kind of world, that open-ended, magical sort of universe where the supernatural is liable to break in at any moment. Our world is an indisputably scientific one, a world tightly governed by rational, experimentally verifiable laws. And as for angels, they just do not fit in.

This absence of angels is due, in other words, to a clear and compelling presence, the presence of predictability. What were the angels, after all, but glorified message boys? The original Greek word *angelos* signifies simply that, a messenger. They arrived on the scene in order to tell people what was going on, what was about to happen. Today, however, we know only too well what is going to happen. What could an angel possibly tell us about the year that lies ahead that we don't already know? Clocks will still tick, and calendars will flip. Money will continue to change hands, and simultaneously lose value. Books will be written—a few will even be read. Banks will be robbed, both with masks and guns, and with computers, smart phones, and all kinds of high-tech. trickery. Oil will dwindle in supply and rise in price. Food supplies will go on accumulating most where they are needed least. Guns, tanks, bombs will still dominate the best-seller lists. And the various churches will issue statements deploring all this, and urging that something be done by someone before it is too late.

Predictability reigns also in our personal lives. New Year resolutions will again be made, and all too swiftly abandoned. Body weight will accumulate, as usual, precisely where it is most visible. Work will continue to drive folk apart in competition, rather than together in cooperation. Bills will have to be paid, letters written, projects proposed, projects completed. Children must be clothed, fed, educated, somehow lived with without losing sight of love altogether. Marriages, relationships will crumble, or be held together by the daily chores of sharing and worrying, quarreling and making up. Gardens will be planted and harvested, vacations planned and taken. Sickness will come and go, one way or the other. Funerals will have to be attended, flowers purchased for new babies, and for old companions.

The confining, crushing, presence of predictability. The secure but deadly knowledge that all this has gone on for a long time now, and will continue to go on for as far ahead as we can foresee, unless someone presses the wrong button and the whole thing stops going on and goes up instead! Where can we find room for angels here? What on earth—or in heaven either—could an angel possibly tell us that would make the slightest difference to the measured, calculated, orderly-if-insane routines of life here in this already-elderly twenty-first century?

Yet is all this really so surprising, so completely new? What is it convinces us that our present era in its predictability, its so-called scientific certainties, is quite so unique? The computer may have been lacking two thousand years ago, but the great computer of the heavens, the inexorable cycle of the seasons, tides, winds, sunrise, sunset, birth, death, mouths to be fed—all these provided their own equally predictable routines. Look back to that first Christmas again. What could have been more foreseeable than the birth of a peasant baby, of doubtful parentage, in a dingy cowshed? The same thing had happened a thousand times before, was going to happen at least a thousand times afterwards. How commonplace can you get, how ordinary, how dull, how routine? Yet this is where we believe it all began. And here is where we begin to learn why it is we see no angels anymore. Because we have been looking for them in the wrong place.

We focus our eyes today on the spectacular, the far-out, the extraordinary. We wait for the drums to roll, the cymbals to clash, the heavens to open. There *was* a heavenly fanfare to be sure; but what's the use of a fanfare sounded so far out into the hills that only a handful of sleepy shepherds can hear? The story of our faith begins right at the heart of things-as-they-are, with a census and taxation, an overflowing inn, a pregnant young wife with an anxious husband, a ruthless ruler, and a murderous militia. Nothing there out of the ordinary, nothing to break the routine, stop the yawn, nothing that could possibly be called unpredictable.

Yet the message of Christmas is that in this most quotidian series of events, if we will look up, we will see angels; we will see our God being born into his world. It is the genius, the uniqueness, of our gospel that it takes its form, puts on its flesh, our God comes to be with us, not in any world-shattering, mind-boggling display of supernatural power, but in the quiet, obscure birth of a hungry baby, in a country town, in an occupied land, in a century that seemed just as predictable as all the rest, including our own. This is the ordinary, everyday, eternal message of the angels.

Therefore, if you would look up and see angels this Christmas; if you would catch a strain of heavenly music, if you would hear those glorious old words of comfort:

> Be not afraid; for behold I bring you good news of a great
> joy . . . (Luke 2:10).

then take care of the ordinary, cherish the everyday, watch out
precisely for the predictable. In wrapping a gift, trimming a tree,
in grace before meals, walking to church, in caring, daily caring for
those whom you cherish beyond all frustration and pain, in bells
at the doors of department stores, checks to sweet charity, calls
on the lonely and lost, in putting the children to bed with a kiss,
setting the alarm, breathing a prayer, in all the routine moments of
this season of custom and routine, look up for Christmas.

> Look up and raise your heads, because your redemption
> is drawing near (Luke 21:28).

Look up and find your Lord and Savior poised to be born,
right here and now, into this, and every moment that has been
given to you—given to you for life.

Among all the gifts of Christmas, might this be among the
greatest, the vision of God's presence, no longer only high and
holy, transcendent, lifted up, but set down right here among us,
at the innermost heart of all we know, all we love? Might it be this
that is the richest gift of all? No wonder those angels sang! No
wonder those shepherds raced to Bethlehem! No wonder the wise
men knelt in wonder and adored! Now what are you, are we, going
to do?

~

*Lord God, our days, our lives, are hastening on, hastening on
toward that time when all gifts will be opened, all secrets will be
unveiled. Help us now to pause the frantic rush and to listen for
your Word, your Word of hope and promise from on high. In the
quiet may we hear the angels' wings, their glorious song of peace on
earth and genuine goodwill. Amen.*

Friday

Intelligent Design

Set aside your sheer astonishment
at the working mechanisms of the human eye;
these steep channels of the mind wear intricacies
that make our universe itself seem child's play.

All these tight entwining arguments that attempt
to make the case for an intelligence beyond our own
may come perilous close, if we're not careful,
to the mere proving, demonstration of their contrary;
that this gray seething mass we bear above brute shoulders
has the capacity to argue almost anything, and to convince
up to the slimmest shadow of a doubt.

All the while, regarding history's sad tale—
tomorrow's headlines from the slaughterhouse,
nature's regular debacles,
the relentless, heartless, onslaughts of disease—
all this can only seem, at best, inscrutable,
malevolent at worst.

Yet ever and again, this latest turning of the year,
an insistent whisper takes the air, a murmur,
not of intelligence, but of rare, quite brilliant compassion.
A tale of lost and found, of nakedness and strange, rich gifts,
of life arriving, just where least expected,
of hope recaptured in a cradled cry.

And hearts are turned outward again,
minds set to devising all kinds of kind surprises,
hands to bundling signs and gestures of affection,
feet to seeking ways to give away.

So that, whatever it is that truly makes us—
design or sheer dumb luck—awakes from slumber,
remembers, fondly, what it came for in the first place,
and calls us, guides us, leads us gently home.

Nothing For Christmas

That's what I'm asking for this year.
That's how I'm responding to my spouse,
siblings, kids and grandkids too who, once again,
insist upon a list of every single thing
I want for Christmas.

Don't you see, it gets to be that,
after almost eighty of these yearly feasts
of dutiful generosity, there's nothing left to ask for?
Haven't they noticed, no one wears neckties any more,
and even in these northern climes—
and losing/leaving things behind, as I do more and more—
I already own sufficient pairs of gloves,
slippers too, to equip a small platoon,
if not a regiment? In other words, my needs
seem to have shrunk, along with my tall stature,
and the wants I feel belong to the non-material variety.

And so I ask nothing—no single thing for Christmas.
Perhaps an hour, instead, of solitude beside the manger,
a nestled child upon my lap, an opened book,
the radiant warmth of burning logs, one day, at least,
of surcease from these varied, mobile, aches and pains
that linger on to test my well-worn frame,
the old familiar touch of tenderness that says,
"I'm glad you're here, still here, after season upon season
of all life's trial and turmoil." Such are the gifts I seek,
not wrapped and laid below the tree, but hidden just beneath
the passing of these late, and almost holy, days.

LIGHTING THE ADVENT CANDLES

(For Joyce and Judith)

Families are asked to do it,
infants toddling to the front to lisp
responsive affirmations to their parents
and the people in the pews concerning
light in darkness.

You brought a new and different light
to bear upon our litany of hope.
Your participation shed
a gentle, unaccustomed brilliance
across all that we have meant by family,
household, living in a lifelong bond
of trust and full commitment.

The candle that you lit will—I pray—
not soon go out but, beating back the dark,
will light a path to recognizing family
wherever love binds past and future
tight within the radiant embrace
of an insistent, broad, and honest grace.

IT'S ABOUT TIME

We're supposed to wait, this time of year,
expectant and anticipating,
maybe even holding our collective breath,
to see what someone, somewhere, has in store,
and is about to be revealed, released,
let loose upon the world.
But I've been waiting now
three-quarters of a century and more,
and days are dwindling at a most alarming rate.

Maybe—ready or not—it's time to just begin,
to let the cat out of the bag,
the child out of the lowly cattle shed,
the gentle gesture, warming welcome,
open calendar and check book,
heart and will unfettered
from precaution and drab fear,
to let them all run free at last.
Then see what might be heading down the pike.

Saturday

GIFTS OF ADVENT III
Company

And many peoples shall come, and say: "Come, let us go up to the mountain of the Lord . . ."

—ISAIAH 2:3

He came to his own home, and his own people received him not. But to all who received him, who believed in his name, he gave power to become children of God . . .

—JOHN 1:11

First, a story. It was Christmas Eve in the year 1353. Europe was held captive in the terrifying grip of the bubonic plague—the Black Death, as it was known. In the tiny German hamlet of Goldberg the streets were deserted, as they had been for many long weeks. No one was moving about. No one was going anywhere. No one even ventured across their threshold for fear that a touch, a cough, even a passing glance, could lead to sudden, agonizing death. One person, however, was determined to observe the feast of Christmas, whether or not he had to do so entirely on his own. Unbarring his great wooden door he strode out onto the village's one street, singing as he went an old Christmas carol—the *Marienlied*—remembered from earlier days. After a few minutes he thought he caught the sound of a second voice, faint, but there just the same. And another door was unbarred, and his company was doubled. As they walked and sang through the village, still other doors were opened, still other voices joined their song, until some twenty-five men, women, and children were gathered, singing together on the *Niederring*, the hill alongside their town.

Who knows? Perhaps it was the song, perhaps the sheer courage and faith of these few scattered survivors, but from that day the plague abated, and the village was saved. And for centuries afterwards the townsfolk of Goldberg marched together to the *Niederring* each and every Christmas Eve, singing their beloved old song:

> To us this day is born a child.
> God with us.
> His mother is a virgin mild.
> God with us. God with us.
> Against us who dare be?

There is nothing like Christmas for company, for calling people, bringing people together.

But we do not have to go all the way back to the Middle Ages. Look around you in church next Sunday morning, take a stroll up Main Street later today, or try any bus depot, railroad station, or airport over the next two weeks, and you will find ample proof that if there is one thing people have at Christmas time, one gift we can be fairly sure of this Advent, it is the gift of company. We're all having company for Christmas.

For most, of course, this is just fine. We wouldn't have it any other way. That's what this cherished season revolves around, family, friends, parties, reunions. Christmas is a magnificent time for simply getting together, for all the convivial, companionable joys we find in human fellowship. But there is more to it than that, more to this gift of company than just another chance for the old gang to gather and swap memories, laughs and the latest stories. Those Christmas cards for one thing, arriving from every corner of the country, of the globe, remind us of a wider company with whom we also share this time of year. And those annual stories in the media with datelines, Bethlehem, Jerusalem, London, Rome, remind us of an even broader company yet, this entire family of God to which we all belong.

One memorable holiday season during our years in New York City, Mhairi, my wife, and I attended our first ever Hanukkah Puppet Show in the apartment of our twelfth-floor neighbor. As we gloried in the color and spectacle—our neighbor was the granddaughter of Marc Chagall and puppets and sets were her own creation—we also took part in a story, a sacred story. This was a story not really our own, yet surely still a part of the family story—those archives and traditions that make of us much more than just a clump of warring clans competing for survival. As that simple, yet profound little play progressed we began to realize that we did belong after all. And when the children broke into cheers and applause at the miracle of the temple lights, we were there too, applauding as vigorously as anyone. We had become convinced that we were part and parcel of it all, that the liberation of the Maccabees, the miraculous deliverance of the Jewish people, was in some way also our deliverance, part of our common heritage, our common hope in God. Yes, in this Advent season we remember the company, this whole world family of which we are a part. We're all having company for Christmas.

There are other companies however, other fellow pilgrims who may not come so easily to mind, or be so readily welcomed. We are reminded in the Scriptures that the one whose coming we anticipate was born an outcast child, far from home, without a decent roof over his head, and was soon to become a refugee in far off Egypt. And so this gift of company, whether we like it or not, brings to us also those who have *no* company, no family or friends to welcome. There are the homeless, the runaway children on our city streets living by drugs and prostitution, easy targets for the scourge of AIDS and other perils. There are the illegal immigrants in search of survival or a better life, flooding the borders of this land and of southern Europe. There are the gypsy peoples of the world, the Romany, so much like Jesus, with no place, no place on earth to call their own. These too are part of our company. These too belong within the family. And unless we can begin to open up our cheery firesides, our elegantly decorated trees, our fearful hearts that wither and die for want of just such openness, then our company this Advent will lack the one element that makes it more than just a huddling together for warmth, and that is compassion.

A well-known journalist, a couple of Decembers ago, in her weekly column in the *New York Times*, told of a different kind of Christmas gift she was giving to her husband. Instead of sweaters, gloves, pajamas—stuff he admitted he neither wanted nor needed—she pledged to cook each week for a homeless shelter run by his favorite charity. As time went by they even began to cook enough so they could travel with the food and join the recipients in their meal. This "Personal Health" article went on to suggest something quite amazing, that according to scientific studies such volunteering can actually be good for a person, can bring about dramatic improvement in one's emotional, even one's physical health. Startling news indeed! What a novel discovery! I guess they never heard the tale of Ebenezer Scrooge, or of another quite some time before, who taught on more than one occasion:

> The one who saves his life, fearfully hoards it up, will surely lose it. While the one who gives life away, has the courage to open up her life to others, will save it for all eternity (Matt 10:39, 16:25; Mark 8:35; Luke 9:24).

Advent brings the gift of company, recalls us to the family, all those who walk this pilgrim way on every side around us. Yet, in our time it often seems that this precious gift is an endangered one, a gift in peril of being forfeited and lost. There appears to be little or no trust left in our society. The triple threat of violence, disease, and litigation has torn the age-old fabric of community, shredded it from top to bottom. We have become fearful of one another: afraid of fellow drivers on the road, or riders in the air or on the rails; afraid of falling in love because of the threat of dire disease, afraid of reaching out to help, or getting involved in any way, for fear we might end up in court despite the best of intentions. Any Good Samaritan on today's Jericho road would first call his lawyer on his iPhone, before checking out the body in the ditch. We live in a cautious, cold, new world, where everyone is suspect, everyone a potential abuser, or potential victim.

Might all this be pointing, however, to a vital role for the church as a place where people can learn to trust again, to share, and even risk again? Much of the potential already exists, I believe, for congregations to nurture communities of basic openness, communities drawn from varied races, ages, backgrounds, educations, and income levels. These would be gatherings of those who, in spite of their differences, dare to spend time together, to share a common dream, a common realization of failure, a common awareness of grace, a common purpose to show forth the acceptance that God has shown in Jesus Christ. Such communities might yet constitute the glimmer of light that brings new hope to many folk who dwell in darkness.

During those fearful Dark Ages we began with today, when everyone in Europe seemed to be for him or herself alone and survival at all costs was the name of the game, the monasteries turned out to be the places that kept civilization alive. They sheltered travelers, cared for the poor, the orphans, the sick, halt, and blind; they preserved the books, the crafts, the healing arts, the melodies, the accumulated wisdom, grace and culture of earlier, brighter ages. And they did this in the name of the Christ who turned no one away.

In these latter days, when the nuclear terror has been replaced by dangers much more intimate, much more close at hand, it often feels as though we are descending into a new Dark Age. Let us, at least, within our churches, seek to preserve that precious gift of trust that lies at the heart of all genuine community, that helping hand, that fundamental bias toward looking for the best in one another and not the worst. We are all of us sinners, sinners saved by grace; but in that grace, and through the cross, we know that we are also, every one of us, a precious child of God, bought at the price of Christ himself, redeemed to live in freedom and as children of the light. We're having company for Christmas. We're *being* company for Christmas.

There is one final sense of company that speaks to us this Advent; for company, in its fullest sense, is what Christmas—the nativity of the Christ—comes down to in the end. God joined *our* company at Christmas. To a human race that was lonely, lost in the mire and fog of sin, and wandered far from home, the God of all creation, Lord of the Universe, Almighty King of Kings, did not merely send a lovely message of peace with his angelic choir. God did not simply provide a star to bring more light and guidance. God did not even issue a blanket pardon, total amnesty for all from the heavenly court on high. God—in a mystery we will never fully comprehend—came himself to save us. That is what incarnation truly means, not just a cute little infant with a halo in a sanitized cowshed, surrounded by reverently kneeling farm animals. All these are just the trappings we have added, added perhaps to shield our eyes from the dazzling truth.

While visiting Saint George's Chapel in Windsor Castle several years ago I saw something that brought a richer, fuller meaning to all this. We stood there almost overwhelmed, taking in the glorious windows, the tombs of kings, queens, and princes, the transcendent soaring pillars—it's still a miracle the way those craftsmen could shape stone until it seemed to take on wings—and up above it all that spectacular fan-vaulted ceiling with its delicate, interwoven tracery. Then, over by the west door I think it was, I noticed a great mirror set low upon a table so that, instead of craning our necks to catch the splendor above, we could look down and marvel at the loveliness reflected there.

And in that mirror I caught a parable of Christmas. The glory that was so distant from us came down to lie at our feet. That divine wonder and beauty that we could perceive only faintly, indistinctly, from afar, drew near, draws near and offers itself before our wondering eyes. God joined our company that first Christmas Eve, broke through the distant, separating clouds of mystery and transcendence, overcame who knows what barriers of divine reluctance, hesitation, even fear. God came out of isolation that first Christmas Eve, opened up the door and walked right through this plague-afflicted village of our world singing his song:

To us this day is born a child.
God with us.
His mother is a virgin mild.

God with us. God with us.
Against us who dare be?

And to all who hear the song, open the door, and join him in his walk, the Lord has promised healing, blessing, joy, and life renewed forever. What a story! What a God!

So let us in these days of Advent that remain rejoice in this gift of company, in all the Christmas wonder of family, friendship, fireside, and fun. But let us not forget that wider company we share, so that we expand our circle to include those who need *our* company in order to survive. Above all, let us remember the truest meaning of this feast, that God has joined our company, that in Immanuel—God with us—our God has set his love beside us, among us, within us, in one grace-filled human life, and through that life has called us to his company forever.

Lord, widen the boundaries we set about this season, open up our days, our lives, our hearts, to the alien, to the lost, to the needy in our midst, to your living presence there to be discovered in the face of all who want. Amen.

Advent Week Four

Sunday

SOMETHING FOR CHRISTMAS IV
Something Worth Living For

In him was life, and the life was the light of all people. The light shines in the darkness, and the darkness has not overcome it.

—JOHN 1:4–5

Triage is a terrible business, demanding soul-wrenching decisions. A Thanksgiving Day human interest story in the newspaper tells of such a decision. The scene, a military evacuation hospital in Pleiku, Vietnam, 1968. A young doctor moves among the newly arrived patients separating, as he must, those who can still be treated, from those beyond all treatment. He comes upon a nineteen-year-old boy, both legs blown away, extensive head wounds, eyes severely damaged and, against all professional judgment, devotes nine hours, the skills of five specialists, to save this young life.

Later he hears that the boy actually made it back to the U.S. but, for years, the physician is plagued with the fear that he made a dreadful mistake, that the remnant of a life he had preserved was, in all probability, being eked out in despair, or perhaps had already been ended by the patient's own hand. Finally the doctor decided to try to discover what had happened. He eventually located the young man and was reunited with him. And the person he met turned out to be a blind, double-amputee who had, in the meantime, married, fathered two children, completed two years of college, taught himself to play piano and trumpet, and learned to sail and scuba dive. It was a humbling moment for that doctor as he realized that his own efforts had been only the beginning, that God and the patient together had brought forth something of a miracle, a remarkably resilient young man with a truly meaningful life before him.

Something worth living for, that's what that young soldier finally found, that's what you and I still seek, I suspect, in all our Christmas busyness of buying, giving, and receiving. Something worth living for.

A few summers ago I visited England's Coventry Cathedral. The historic old sanctuary had been reduced almost to rubble by one of the most devastating bombing raids of World War II. When the time came to rebuild, however, a truly inspired decision was made, a decision not to tear down those shattered walls and broken window arches, but to preserve them and erect the new cathedral by their side. As you enter that great house of God today the wreckage of the older building, all the debris of human pride, greed and violence, stands about you, a tragic reminder, inescapably visible through the great, clear-glass west windows. Inside, suspended above the high altar, a vast tapestry of the risen Christ, hands raised in benediction, shines through the glass and out onto the ruins beyond. And that transparent glass is etched all over with images of saints, angels, mothers, and fathers in the faith.

And then it dawns; the message of those buildings, their design and their placement, strikes with the power of revelation. The risen Lord shines through the holy ones, the believers of all ages, through folk like you and me, out into the tragic chaos of our world. And this broken world sees through to Christ, perceives, receives the blessing and the healing only he can bring, by way of those same holy ones, the believers of all times and places, who seek and struggle, strive to live the faith that came to earth that first Christmas Eve. Something to live for.

Have you ever sat in church, close to midnight Christmas Eve, and gazed up at the stained glass windows? It's a disappointing moment, really, because there is nothing to be seen. Without the radiant light of the sun streaming through their multicolored panes church windows can only appear dark and lifeless. But if you were to step outside that church, venture into the bitter cold, pitch black of the December night, then you would see a sight not soon forgotten. For as you view them from the darkness, as they catch, reflect, send forth the light within, those windows shine with a wonder richer far than any you will see by daylight. Even so, the true glory of our Christmas faith is fully caught only when viewed against the darkness of this world. The truest message of that holiest of nights is only heard when transmitted through the inner radiance of folk like you and me, folk who seek to make that message of "Peace on earth, goodwill to all" a living, breathing reality shining far into the darkest corners of our world. "In him was life," wrote John:

> In him was life, and the life was the light of all people.
> The light shines in the darkness, and the darkness has not overcome it.

Something worth living for.

Almost fifteen years ago now I traveled back to New York City, just a few days after what has now come to be known as "9/11," to take part in the installation service of my successor at The First Presbyterian Church in the City of New York. The church had suffered the loss of eight faithful and beloved members in that attack, as well as a number of close friends and neighbors. I visited the site—Ground Zero—trod through the lingering dust, smelled the acrid smoke, tasted the ash still hanging in the air, prayed on the edge of the abyss with rescue workers, police, and soldiers in old Saint Paul's Chapel. Here is something of what I said in my sermon soon afterwards:

> To put it at its simplest, we live with two realities, two towering cosmic facts that stare us in the face, dominate our living, either by their presence or their absence. The one is love, the other, death. All the rest is strategy. And the question is, the question always is, which one wins. Which one triumphs in the end? Which one is God?
>
> If death is God, then those nineteen fanatics won. Then, in a very real sense, there is nothing left to live for. Then you, your precious life, however many days are left

before the lightbulb hits the concrete floor, before the towers come crashing down, these are the only things that count, and everything else, everyone else, becomes negotiable . . . if death is God.

If love is God, on the other hand, if love is the power that wins out in the end, then everything is possible. If love is God, if nothing is to be feared but fear itself, and we have one who has conquered fear by his own broken body given for our sakes, if that love that Jesus demonstrated on the cross beats at the heart of everything that is, and moves it, not toward a frigid, bleak extinction of eternal winter, but toward a springtime destiny beyond the stars, then we are ultimately, cosmically liberated, set free for living, for pouring out our lives, as he did, for the sake of others, and thus discovering, perhaps for the very first time, just who we really are, our own true and best, our immortal selves.

Something worth living for.

Here is the truest hope of Christmas, the genuine power behind all we will celebrate on this, and every Christmas Eve. Beyond the cathedral walls and windows, within both the terror and the beauty of this world, there lies that something that *is* worth living for. And that something is love. Love that can take our ordinary daily lives and shine clear through them and out into a hurting, yet still hoping world with the radiance of Christ. Love that reveals to us the family of God in the eyes of each person we meet.

The calendar has moved along. In this last week before Christmas this world of ours will turn back toward the light. The days will start to grow longer again. The hours of dark and cold will grow shorter. And so it will continue until springtime. This world of ours is turning itself toward the light. Will we? Can we kneel beside the humble stall, receive the light, the tender, fragile, yet eternally enduring light, into our darkened, fearful hearts, and then go forth to show its richness wherever there is hurt or fear or want? Something worth living for.

~

As this wintered world turns itself toward the light, toward spring-time and the renewal of life, even so turn us toward the inner light, that light that is eternal, the living Word that comes to rest here in our midst this holy, gracious, season of the year. Amen.

Monday

An Advent Prayer for Immanuel—
God With Us

O Come, O Come, Immanuel.
How can we forget, Lord,
how can we forget that you have already come,
that you came to your own, and your own received you not,
that you came with arms outstretched in love,
and we stretched them out again, this time in pain,
and hammered nails through them,
that you came bearing the gift of eternal life,
and we chose death,
have gone on choosing death until this very day?
O Come, O Come Immanuel—God With Us.

O Come, O Come, Immanuel.
How can we not see, Lord,
how can we not see that you do still come,
that, despite our past rejection, you come to us here and now
in the presence of our fellow humankind, their gifts,
their rich blessings, their cries for help,
you are present in the needs of this world,
in the challenges of this moment, in insight, imagination,
and peace, in lostness, fear, and despair,
and all of this with grace,
grace that is both a comfort and a call?
O Come, O Come, Immanuel—God With Us.

O Come, O Come, Immanuel.
How can we not hope, Lord,
how can we not hope? This is your creation,

molded with your hands, brought to life with your breath,
wept over with your tears, redeemed with your own blood.
As you have brought it into being, so one day
you will bring it to its end, in glory and in grace,
in majesty and in mystery, in a full cosmic restoration
of beauty, truth and love.
Prepare us now for that final restoration.
Open us to beauty, ground us in truth, fill us with self-giving,
that having known you in our past, and seeing you now
in our present, we might find hope for the future in you.
O Come, O Come, Immanuel—God With Us.

THE COMING OF THE LIGHT

A
pure
and
golden
light, it
seems, that
spreads across
the pews, reflects
its radiance from the
mellow old carved oak
and hanging greens upon
the faces, hands of those
who sing so sweetly
"Silent Night." Look deep
into this gentle fire
and then go forth to bear
it, far and tender, to
wherever infants, cold
and frightened, tremble
in the dark with
no bright star
no kings
to
greet.

Have Seen a Great Light

It's all the little lights we love
this darkening season of the year,
those miniature illuminations crafted tiny-tight,
to twinkle, delicate among the branches
of the fragrant pine, or balsam fir,
attempting to evoke, perhaps, the far-flung mystery
of galaxies, spread like a glistening garment
full across the shadowed velvet vault.

This great and dazzling light,
foreseen by seers and prophets, seems
too bright and glaring for our modern sight,
even in these blaring times. This present darkness
seems to yield more readily to subtlety, suggestion,
to the gentle, yet persistent glow that spills
across the ages, from the radiance
that gathers past Andromeda.

The Messiah

A lilt on the lips

        a fiddle for the feet

                a humming in the heart

       a tap to the toes

a music for the mind

                a spring for the soul

Thank you, Lord,

       and Mister Handel!

Tuesday

How Many Miles to Bethlehem? IV
The Destination

O house of Jacob,
come, let us walk
in the light of the Lord.

—Isaiah 2:5

Former New York Governor Hugh Carey, in an interview deep into his retirement years, had been reflecting on his long and powerful political career. But, at the close, he turned to thoughts of family and friends, his everyday routine, his early morning walk which ended up at daily Mass in a nearby sanctuary. "Not a bad way to kick your day off." Carey commented. And then he added, "I figure as I'm getting to the evening of my life, I'm beginning to pack my bags for the journey." We too have been looking at the journey over the past three weeks, this Advent journey to Bethlehem, packing *our* bags for whatever lies ahead. This morning, as the days count swiftly down, we look ahead to the destination.

That very first Advent journey, as has already been suggested, was not the solitary affair that we like to portray on our Christmas cards. In all likelihood the holy couple traveled, for security, in a caravan with many others. Bethlehem was the final stopping place on the highway to Israel's capital, Jerusalem. Therefore it's not too difficult to visualize their companions on the way. There would be merchants with them, headed for the capital on business, out to make a living, perhaps even a killing, in the wool, spice, or cattle trade. Soldiers too, I should imagine, were there on that busy road, marching under orders, ready for the slaughter of infants, should such become necessary, in order to preserve the precious *Pax Romana*. Tax collectors would almost certainly be there, ferrying their blood money back to the Roman authorities. Ordinary citizens must have been there too, complying with Caesar's decree that they be registered for still further taxation. Even, just a bit later, shepherds and magi were to be seen on that road, seeking a newborn king. Many travelers then, and each to their own journey, each to their own destination. What about us, as we make our own wayfaring ways toward Bethlehem, distracted by all the demands, desires, diversions of this over-scheduled time of year? Which direction are we headed in? Which destination have we selected for ourselves?

There are those who insist that there are two, and only two, possible destinations. We are either headed up or headed down, destined—perhaps even predestined—for heaven or for hell. Yet, for my own part, any religion that has to resort to scaring folk toward God has already abandoned its fundamental purpose. Any religion that raises children in the dread of an eternal lake of fire is guilty of spiritual child abuse, not to mention sacrilege against a God who so loved his children that he gave up his only son for their sakes. Novelist Morris West has written somewhere that God wants us running toward him like lovers, not stampeded like a herd of terrified cattle.

I read recently of someone who was challenged to set down our basic Christian theology in twenty words or less. Here's what she came up with:

> God said, "I'm going to love you sinners even if it kills me." It did. He still does.

A pretty fair summary. It leaves lots of room for mercy, and that "amazing" grace folk love to sing about. It even leaves two words to spare.

What *is* our destination? There are those of us—better say, there is that in many of us, myself included—that views our journey as one headed toward success. We have been outfitted with the finest in traveling equipment: a well-rounded upbringing, excellent education, top-drawer family, acquaintances, contacts, networks, so that we are already a fair distance along the road, maybe even within sight of the goal. Others may be just starting out, or gathering provisions for the route, while still others may have experienced a setback, a promotion that slipped by, a job change, health change, marriage coming apart. Even so we're on the march, marking time for now perhaps, but ready as soon as possible to resume that sure and steady progress. There is the destination called "success," with Christmas, on this route, merely another opportunity to display how far we've already come, to trim a glittering tree with all the splendid trophies we've amassed.

For others of us, and within all of us at some point, there is the journey toward pleasure, with life seen as a quest for satisfaction, sensation, the very latest thrill, toy, or show, the hottest restaurant, finest wine, most lavish cruise, escape-from-winter getaway. For some this takes the form of the quest for new frontiers in sex or substances that blow the mind. But pleasure is a drive we all share—just check the glossy magazines this time of year, any time of year for that matter. This journey has its characteristic Christmas also. Not "Silent Night" but "Swinging Night," a blast, a frolic, revelry, in what they call "the true spirit of this gala season."

Browsing the bookstore displays I picked up a pretty little booklet entitled *Christmas in New York* that informed me that New York is "the center of the universe" during the holiday season and went on to describe all the delightful ways to be a part of it. There are chapters, as you might imagine, on "Museums," "Shows and Spectacles," "Macy's Thanksgiving Day Parade," "Santa-ology" and "A Tour of the Shop Windows on Fifth Avenue." As for the churches, as for opportunities for worship during this ostensibly Christian festival, apart from two or three lines on how to obtain tickets for Midnight Mass at Saint Patrick's, they were conspicuously absent. Religion, God, the Babe of Bethlehem himself found no room at the inn, or at "the center of the universe" of *Christmas in New York*. One may select that destination called pleasure.

There are others who travel somberly along that pathway that leads toward the grave. These weather-beaten voyagers have seen far beyond the reaching for success, a reaching ever doomed to failure, if for no other reason than because there can never be enough of it. They have seen clear through the shimmering mirage of pleasure as the pursuit of momentary passions which, the moment they are tasted turn to ashes in the mouth. With bitter eye and downturned lip, a cynical facade to mask a shattered spirit, they move along the highway of the years, killing time in pursuits that may anesthetize, for a while, the pointlessness of everything. And Christmas for such world-weary pilgrims is a hollow thing, a humbug, one further reminder of another year gone by. Which journey, which destination are you headed for?

It might be more honest to say that we move back and forth among them all. We vacillate between these destinations, seeking both success *and* satisfaction to mask an all-pervasive pessimism. And like those hardened gamblers at the slots we win just often enough to make us keep on losing. I'm reminded of the tale of the young man, headed for university, who came to seek his minister's blessing. "What are your plans?" the pastor inquired.

"Well, I'm going to enroll in classes that will help me get a job, and make a decent living." the lad responded.

"And then?" said the minister.

"And then, after I graduate and get a job, I plan to settle down and get married."

"And then?"

"Well then, after a while, it will be time to start a family."

"And then?"

"I suppose eventually I'll be able to retire."

"And then?"

"Well, then I guess I'll develop my golf game and my garden."

"And then?"

Addressing a typical audience of upwardly mobile "suits," a best-selling author and social critic pointed out that, while most of them had "done well," their success was woefully inadequate unless they had also "done good."

Journeys and destinations. Which journey are you on, where are you headed for this late Advent, late December morning?

This week, as I have noted, we mark the winter solstice, the hour when earth's orbit shifts, the daylight starts its slow but steady increase, and we begin our homeward journey back toward the sun. This Advent season offers its own turning toward the light, another kind of light, another kind of journey, an alternative destination to these we have just visited. It promises—to be completely honest—little, if any, of the success we have just considered. Mary and Joseph, far from being numbered among the great and the good, the movers and shakers of their time, wound up as refugees, fleeing with their child to far-off Egypt. There's not much pleasure in it either. It certainly may be natural, but it's hardly the most comfortable way to have a baby, delivering it in the straw of a rough-hewn cattle stall.

Yet their journey led to a cradle, not to a grave; it guided them toward birth, and not toward death. Their journey moved toward hope and left despair far behind, a hope that has not faded, as so many do, with time but has echoed and re-echoed for now two thousand years. Their journey led them on toward a mystery, but a mystery in no way malevolent, or menacing, rather one that was as gentle and kind as a newborn baby, yet just as complex, just as demanding, just as inviting.

Sometimes a destination can take us by surprise. We can end up in Bethlehem just when we least expect it. My own destination, one frigid December morning, was a federal maximum security facility. I was on my way to visit a parishioner who had fallen upon harsh and challenging times. After going through the humiliating full-body search required of all visitors, I was seated in the prison waiting area, pondering just how I might communicate the message of Christmas in such an unlikely setting, when I was drawn into conversation with a little child and his young mother sitting across from me. She told me she had driven for hours on icy backroads to make her first visit ever to her father, serving time for drug offenses. She mentioned that her father had never spent a Christmas out of jail in over thirty years; that he had been in prison when she was born and had encouraged her mother to remarry and bring her up in ignorance of his existence. Recently, however, now married and mother of a delightful little boy, she had begun to ask questions, put two and two together, and had finally tracked him down. She told me of her concern to give him, in her son, someone to live for, someone for whom to attempt to turn his life around.

And later, across the crowded, clamorous visitors' lounge, as I watched that grizzled old grandfather clasping to himself his new-found grandson, that beaming, teary-eyed mother talking with her new-discovered dad, I realized that I had glimpsed the Holy Family. In that barren place of guilt and sin, and broken, wasted lives, I found myself kneeling in the straw beside a battered, blessed cattle stall as love tore down all barriers and rejoined life to life in forgiveness, joy, and bright new promise.

Which journey are we on? What does our future hold? Which destination are we headed for?

> O house of Jacob,
> come let us walk
> in the light of the Lord.

So sang the prophet Isaiah. And so let us, in this winter-darkened season, choose once again the way of light. Let us take up that oldest and yet newest journey, that way toward mystery that brings us birth and death, the manger and the cross, and then beyond death, beyond the furthest boundaries of despair, brings life again, gives itself again, gives hope, grace, and love again, for us to take, unwrap the bindings of our wintered lives, and bear it, wear it, put it on forever.

✑

Lead me to the manger, Lord. There let me kneel and find myself
in you. Then lead me forth to walk beside you on your journey
toward peace on earth, goodwill to all. Amen.

Wednesday

GENE THERAPY

And were we built to be this way?
Is there locked in our twin spiral that which leads,
propels us on toward the spilling of that scarlet,
brimming liquid, whose loss endangers life itself?
Need our traveling on in search of birth be ever set
within the probabilities of terror, sudden death?

Must our young forever come to soldiers,
warriors, those who enter without any invitation,
the sole of the hob-nailed boot their calling card,
a cocked and loaded weapon held on high as hostess gift?

And must this annual anticipation of the Prince of Peace
be ever a "despite" affair, a festival we have to hold,
for pity's sake, at arm's length—world's length even—
from the blood-stained evening news?

Or might that child in his defenselessness call forth,
evoke, a deeper impulse yet, an even older primal urge
to stretch forth tender arms, to cradle and caress,
sing lullaby, and nurture with that softest, warm,
most comforting, the earliest and best of all our blessed gifts,
a mother's gentle breast?

WISH

For Christ-mass
  I would like to see
    a real-live mass of Christ-
      ians round this ragged globe
        head over heels in love
          with babes in muddy mangers
            travel-weary wise old men
              and smelly shepherds
                not to mention
                  the odd donkey here and there.

December Eighteen

(Awaiting the First Snowstorm)

Three to five inches,
that's what they're calling for,
overnight into the morning hours.
And tail lights glow as streets and parking lots,
supermarkets too, throng with over-prudent seekers
preparing for disaster, yet again,
secret hoping that perhaps this time
they will actually get to use those candles,
cans of Campbell's, and the jumbo-pack
of extra batteries.

Home, I lower blinds against the dark,
sensing a gathering in the air,
a suspended, swaddling, silence,
pregnant with a multitude shimmering flakes,
ready, despite the accumulated evidence
of seventy-nine past winters,
to be astonished once again,—
surprised almost to kneeling in the gentle stuff—
at what this ordinary, too familiar world
can do with falling water.

Thursday

LOOKING FOR CHRISTMAS IV
Look back for Christmas

. . . remember the former things of old;
for I am God, and there is no other;
I am God, and there is none like me,
declaring the end from the beginning
and from ancient times things not yet done . . .

—ISAIAH 46:9–10

One of the fascinating things about receiving Christmas cards from overseas is that you can begin to spot the trends. Cards from the U.K., for example, used to favor lots of carolers with lanterns in the snow. In recent years, however, the three wise men have been quite definitely "in" over there. Yet this year, while still rather early to make firm predictions, the three kings do seem to be running way behind. Just what this might suggest about the current status of the British monarchy is certainly food for thought!

Spotting trends in the U.S. can be more difficult. But one thing I have noticed, and that is the almost complete unavailability of contemporary Christmas cards. By contemporary I do not mean those elegant calligraphy designs using only lettering, or cards that are variously humorous, or even vulgar. I mean cards bearing contemporary scenes; cards depicting people, not in first-century AD, or Dickensian nineteenth-century garb, but in twenty-first-century dress, doing twenty-first-century things, in a twenty-first-century way. Instead, in our Christmas cards as in our Christmas songs, Christmas customs, even those home-printed Christmas letters that insist on detailing every tooth, every trauma, every triumph over the past twelve months, in so much of what we do this time of year we seem to be looking back, looking backward for Christmas.

Occasionally I find myself wondering if, a century on from now, Christmas cards will bear pictures of jolly families in their antique Toyota or Jeep SUVs, drawing up to the doorways of venerable suburban town houses, or antique McMansions, with old-fashioned, electric lighted trees in the windows, and perhaps a quaint, old snowmobile parked somewhere in the background. We do tend to look backward, ever backward for Christmas.

At one time, not too many years ago, I might have denounced this tendency as an exercise in escapism, a nostalgic attempt to insulate Christmas from the harsh realities of our modern world. Nowadays, however, I am becoming more and more convinced that, to quote a former pastor-neighbor in Greenwich Village: "Relevance is a wonderful servant, but a terrible master." And while it is undoubtedly true that Christ, born in a stable two thousand years ago, is also being born here and now, in a war-torn village in Somalia or Ukraine, a homeless shelter in Chicago, a labor camp in North Korea, it is equally true that if we cannot look back and draw strength from the eternal message of that first Christmas Eve, we will have little of lasting value to say to the tragedies of our own time. Look back for Christmas, then, look back with me this Advent toward Christmas.

When we look back for Christmas I believe we look back, in the first place, in order to find ourselves. For the past is our story, yours and mine. The days of the years of our lives are very much a part of us. We became who we are now back there, back then. It was Tennyson who reminded us that all experience is an arch through which we view the future. Consequently, if we would really know ourselves, be ourselves, live in harmony with our true selves, then we have to look back, look backward for Christmas.

Look back with me now, see a young boy in an industrial city in the north of England carefully unwrapping, through six long years of warfare—an entire remembered childhood in fact— an ever dwindling collection of fragile pre-war ornaments and

Christmas decorations, hanging them on an increasingly tilted artificial tree that was as old as he was and, last of all, the star, that battered, tinseled symbol of enduring hope throughout those dark and dangerous years.

Or see that same young man, years later, in RAF uniform, heading home on leave for the holidays, with a train too late for its connection on Christmas Eve, wandering far out under the stars to the end of the platform at Doncaster station, and glimpsing peace on earth, at least the hope of universal goodwill, that starry, holy night. Or, later still, see him caroling at midnight in the crowded graveyard of a nine-hundred-year-old house of God, or serving the Lord's Supper in a Chicago storefront church that had been, until recently, a corner saloon.

Look back into the stars, and snows, and glowing family firesides, of your own Christmases, and begin to find yourself again, to know yourself, to be yourself again. For we look backward at Christmas, first of all, to find our own true selves.

But still more can be said. For the past is not only my story and yours. It is humanity's story, the record of the ages, all the good, the bad, and the beautiful, that bring us to where we are today. And in looking back for Christmas we look backward also into all of this. Thus we share our Christmas memories, not only with family and friends, but with a wider, far more colorful congregation. We can shed a tear with Charles Dickens over Tiny Tim and Scrooge. We can stalk the arctic cats and cheer the firemen in Mrs. Prothero's parlor with Dylan Thomas. We can catch the dancing, gossamer magic of *The Nutcracker* with Peter Ilyich Tchaikovsky. We can join Leo Tolstoy in a breathless day of hunting, and the sudden, overwhelming hospitality of a rough old country squire. We can soar to "Waken Sleepers" with Johann Sebastian Bach, or sing that "Unto Us a Child is Born" with George Frederick Handel, carol "Venite Adoremus" with the medieval monks and know again the magic of Luke's "For behold, I bring you glad tidings of great joy."

So it is that, looking backward for Christmas, we come to recognize, not only our own selves, but our fellow pilgrims on this universal journey in search of a star, that vast fellowship of dreamers, hopers, believers, who have brightened the long winter by sharing their own glimpses of the light. We look back for Christmas, and we find, once again, that we belong; we belong not only to ourselves but to something far wider and greater, this hurting, hoping, ever dreaming people of God.

For thirdly, as we look back for Christmas, we discover that the past is not just my story, and your story, not even just humanity's story. The past is His story—history we call it—a story that began with Him before all ages, and will end with Him in the wisdom of His eternity. This is a story that broke open into all our stories at a manger with a mother and a child, a world that couldn't care less, and a God who couldn't care more—and was born among us, lived and died to prove it. This is a story of a bleak, harsh journey out of season, of an inn and a stable, shepherds and wise men. This is an old, old story which lives in all our hearts no matter how we deny it, seek to rationalize it away as myth or legend, sugarcoat it over with sticky sentiment or commercial grab-and-greed. It is a story that we would not, maybe even could not, be without.

Imagine for a moment, that we had never found Luke's gospel, or Matthew's. All we had was Mark and John which, for all their drama, theology, and poetry record nothing of the circumstances of Jesus' birth. The Christian faith would survive, to be sure. The immortal words and deeds—Golgotha, the Easter Garden—would still be there. But so much would be lost, so much of tenderness and humility, so much identification with the helpless poor and outcast, the alien and refugee, so much of gentleness and compassion, so much of wonder, mystery and awe. Yes, we would still have the Easter faith; but it would be, for me at least, a thinner faith, a paler, more threadbare, in some indefinable way a poorer faith without this marvelous mystery-of-a-tale of how God came to be with us through the stable door of ordinary human history, through the pregnancy, birth, and nurture of a helpless human infancy.

Looking back, then, for Christmas means above all else, looking back to his unique story. And as we read and hear again those old, familiar, words:

> And it came to pass in those days that a decree went out
> from Caesar Augustus . . . (Luke 2:1).

as we hearken to these syllables of promise, birth and hope, his story becomes a part of our story, of their story, of each and every human story. We become caught up into that story, become a living part of Christmas, witnesses of the mystery, participants in the miracle, worshippers at the manger, bearers of this wondrous child out of the past and into this present moment with its urgent concerns, shrieking headlines, its all-too-relevant demands. And this is so because we have looked back for Christmas, and having done so, having found ourselves in his story, we can look forward again in hope. We can move ahead with confidence. We can begin again to serve this world into which he came, in which he reigns even now in quiet and wonderful ways, this world of which he will make, one day, his own eternal Kingdom, the kingdom of Immanuel—God with us.

≈

As we have looked back for Christmas, so let us now look ahead.
Guide us toward a searching world, a world that more than ever
needs your gentleness, your humility, your quiet, clear compassion.
And let us bear those gifts within our living days, to move this
darkened world toward the everlasting light. Amen.

Friday

INTERMISSION

By the time
that you find time to read this,
most of the usual stuff will have
already happened: cards, calendars
and gifts, melodies, greeneries, long lists
and late night revelries, blinking lights,
parking lots, chairs set around the table,
then set back against the wall.

Stop then.
Find once again the long-lost child
in her, in you—wherever—
that can open up, reveal, display
the still point of this scintillating present,
and then bend the aching knee,
acknowledging, at last,
there's much more to all of this
than meets the eye.

MINIMIZING MAGIC

We celebrate the ordinary in our time,
point out the muddy messiness of stables
and those friendly beasts,
accentuate the workaday of shepherds,
the available astrological expertise of magi,
Mary's unfortunate teenage pregnancy,
and the impact of that winter's journey
on poor Joseph's job security.
All this tells us—we are fond of pointing out—
that Christ can come into our time as well,
that our God is born right at the heart of things
just as they are and always have been.

While all the time
a blazing star and angels,
prostrate, bedazzled shepherds,
amazing, and alarming kings with gifts,
an immaculate, adoring, blue-caped mother,
and an age-old, newborn, God on golden straw
sing wonder to our weary ears, gleam glory to
our bleary eyes, and charm us to that old, eternal
realm where everything is seen shot through
with marvel, mystery and miracle,
and the ordinary disappears,
dissolved into the holy.

Pre-Nativity

December Twenty Third

There had to be a star involved;
stars have ever had that two-edged tendency
toward portending, given half a chance.
Last evening's light-strewn firmament,
spread wide above my own quotidian
bedtime walking with the dogs
reminded me what day it was about to be.
"Tomorrow will be Christmas Eve Eve,"
as I annually informed my patient children years ago,
still do whenever I get the opportunity.

Some find the viewing of our spangled universe
renders them lost, and on the brink of fright,
crushed beneath those swirling magnitudes.
For myself, after almost eighty Decembers
gazing upward into darkly frosted skies,
there remains a certain charged delight,
a spark that travels tight along the spine—
less apprehension than anticipation—
a persistent bright suspicion
that such far-flung loveliness bears more
than dust toward a waiting manger.

Just Asking . . .

Might they have got it wrong,
all those contemplating sages who saw Bethlehem,
the manger child, as the desperate last straw,
God's grudging rolling of the dice when,
after centuries of failure—patriarchs, prophets,
seers and judges, singers of the psalter—
he was compelled, at the bitter end,
to send his one and only son to save us?

What I'm asking, this time round, is,
might this have been the game plan all along,
the cosmic culmination, Eden's actual fulfilment,
and that soaring angel song an earthly echo
of God's pealing laughter and delight
at all that was unfolding here below?

Might it be that God shared
in our wonder at the stable and the straw,
the sheer earthiness of everything,
that final, everlasting affirmation
that even God,
yes, even God belongs?

Saturday

GIFTS OF ADVENT IV
Song

And the ransomed of the Lord shall return,
and come to Zion with singing;
everlasting joy shall be upon their heads;
they shall obtain joy and gladness,
and sorrow and sighing shall flee away.

—ISAIAH 35:10

. . . be filled with the Spirit, addressing one another in psalms and
hymns and spiritual songs, singing and making melody to the Lord
with all your heart . . .

—EPHESIANS 5:18-19

Sixty-three winters ago, in the early years of the Cold War, a group of servicemen in the British Royal Air Force were tramping home to their bomber base on a crisp early December evening, their heels ringing on the cobblestones of a tree-lined lane in Lincolnshire. They were returning from choir practice in the tiny, nearby village church, where they had been rehearsing for *The Messiah*, a long and cherished tradition in that corner of rural England. Spontaneously the lads began to sing together as they walked:

> For unto us a child is born,
>
> unto us a son is given,
>
> And the government shall be upon his shoulder.

And the velvet sky, vivid with frosted stars, echoed their young, strong, voices. I've never forgotten that Sunday evening walk, the clear beauty and poignancy of that moment, caught in time, and yet beyond all time. It sings to me yet of youth, of faith and hope, and of the rich expectation of this Advent season.

This is, of all times, a season for singing, and in churches, high school auditoriums, famous concert halls, street corners too across the globe, voices are being raised in a host of familiar and cherished melodies. Kathleen Norris, in her best-selling book, *The Cloister Walk*, writes:

> Church meant two things to me when I was little: dressing up and singing. I sang in choirs from the time I was four years old and for a long time believed that singing was the purpose of religion . . .[1]

What is it about singing, what is it about music, that links it, binds it, weaves it all across, around and through our Christian faith, for it has been there from the very beginning? The writer of the book of Job has it that when God created the heavens and the earth:

> . . . the morning stars sang together,
> and all the children of God shouted for joy . . . (Job 38:7).

And from those angelic choirs above the shepherds of Bethlehem, to the hymn sung by the disciples at the close of the Last Supper, to the songs of faith of the early church incorporated into our New Testament and those mighty chorales of the book of Revelation, music has been an essential element in all that we have been, all that we still are today. Let me suggest three reasons why this is so, why song and singing are among the most beloved, the most appreciated gifts of Advent. First I would propose that music lifts us.

The joining in a hymn, the chanting of a choir, introits, anthems, processionals, recessionals, all of these are designed to take us out of ourselves. They have the ability to elevate us, even if only

---

1. Norris, *The Cloister Walk*, 90.

for a moment, far above the daily stuff of diaries and deadlines, everything that drags us down, all the weighty stuff that keeps us grounded, tethered, moored to solid and unyielding earth. When we sing together, or even when we give rapt attention to the music-making of others, we lay aside our burdens and participate in something timeless, something beautiful, something indefinably grace-filled and true. So that when we have to take them up again—these daily chores, details, and duties—we find that they are lighter, just a bit, or perhaps that we are more able now to cope with them, to bear them.

They claim that as long as you are self-conscious it is almost impossible to sing. You tell yourself you have a dreadful voice, and that everyone will be looking at you, wishing you would go away, or at least be quiet. So you stand there feeling miserably alone, deprived, left out. But if you can forget yourself, become, as it were, self-*un*conscious, then whatever your voice, you lose yourself, and it too, in something vaster, grander, truer than you could ever achieve alone. And you are making music. Or might it be that music is making you?

And that leads into my second thought. For as we join in song we find that music not only lifts us, it also links us. Music dissolves the fearful fences, all the protective walls we build up around ourselves, and leads us gently outward into chorus, into community, into congregation. Our voices, no matter how inexperienced or proficient, contrive to blend, are taken up by the melody itself, and then shaped into a harmony that transcends individual gifts and contributions and creates something quite new.

Music links us, not just with those about us in the present, but with those who have gone before, with parents, grandparents, teachers, those who taught us these songs from the beginning; and with Palestrina, Mozart, and Hildegard of Bingen, with the monks and their Gregorian, the Puritans and their solemn, austere psalms. And so we join that vast community of song linked by all those musical expressions of our faith that go beyond mere words and have the power to move us, if we're not careful, to the depths of our being.

I have shared my own love for music throughout most of my life with my younger brother, Dick. We were both keen amateur musicians, playing cornet in brass bands together, singing together in choral groups and church choirs. Dick beat me to the finish line a couple of years ago and, as a fitting memorial, Mhairi and I donated a collection of anthems for the Advent season to the church choir he sang in back in Scotland. Now, each December, those cherished melodies and harmonies renew the bonds we forged over almost seventy years of making a joyful sound to the Lord together, and we are linked in the great, harmonious communion of saints.

Music links us, it brings us, binds us together in other ways as well. Music can help dissolve barriers; it can assist us to communicate with each other, and to communicate on levels not available in the realm of the purely and exclusively verbal. Witness the tale of the man who wrote to Albert Einstein requesting that the great scientist describe his theory of relativity in simple everyday terms, so that he might be able to explain it to his grandchildren. Einstein is said to have responded that he was unable to comply with the request—relativity being far too complex a theory to be reduced in such a way. However, rather than disappoint his inquirer completely, he would be willing to have him stop by his home in Princeton where he would play the theory for him on his violin. Music helps us to communicate on levels far beyond the merely verbal.

Music lifts us, then, music links us, and thirdly, music lights our way home. I cannot tell you how many times people—friends, parishioners, colleagues—have said to me, "Now remember, please, I want that hymn sung . . . I want that anthem performed by the choir . . . I want that piece of music played at my funeral." For music links us, not just to each other and to the past of faith, but to the future, and our future hope. It is really no surprise that the book of Revelation overflows with hymns, or that the angels are regularly depicted with harps in their hands. As we are lifted up in music we gain new perspective on the way ahead; we glimpse the far horizons and beyond; we sense that there is more to life than this, more than just the daily grind, the relentless race to stay even. When we sing we learn to look ahead and to rejoice in what we see there.

That song we sang so many Decembers ago now, that long-remembered chorus from *Messiah* along that frosty Lincolnshire lane, "For unto us a child is born . . ." goes on to sing, "And his name shall be called, 'Wonderful!'" And that last word, "Wonderful," sounds forth like a great clash of cymbals or a mighty trumpet fanfare, because that's just what this gift of song, this splendid season for singing can restore, can give back to us, that precious, all too fragile sense of wonder.

On a visit to England's Durham Cathedral I found myself in the Galilee Cloister among the tombs of the early saints, Cuthbert and The Venerable Bede among them. As I stood there, contemplating the high and holy mysteries that surround one in such a spot, the soaring music of the cathedral choir echoing around me lifting, linking, lighting my way, I called to mind a tale that is told of those earliest Celtic monks. It seems one of those bold preachers of Christ's gospel stood in the court of one of the early kings and, after hearing him all that long day, the ruler, surrounded by his thanes and counselors, would ask that preacher just one question, one vital inquiry.

If I become Christ's man what will I find? What will I find?

If you become his liege—was the answer—If you become Christ's man,

you will find wonder upon wonder, and every wonder true.

And his name shall be called . . . *Wonderful!* A song that lifts us. A song that links us. A song that lights our Advent way.

∽

*Blend my voice, Lord—not just my voice, but my very being—
weave me into the song you sing, the glorious hymn of all creation,
the music of the spheres. Then let me find my place, and sing my
part, with all the life that is in me. And may it be ever to your
glory, world without end. Amen.*

Christmas Eve

Room for Christmas

And she gave birth to her first born son and wrapped him in swaddling cloths, and laid him in a manger, because there was no room for them in the inn.

—Luke 2:7

Home for the holidays. Magical words. Warm, well-rounded words. Words that express so much of the meaning of Christmas. Home, home for the holidays.

A print by Currier and Ives: the sleigh is drawn up at the foot of the farmhouse steps, an open door frames a candle-bedecked tree, warmly clad youngsters leap into the arms of grandparents, parents still wrapped in rugs and furs, clasping hands, smiling, patient horses breathing mist on the frosty air, holly wreaths on doors, lighted candles in each window, snow everywhere, and you can almost smell those fresh-baked apple pies. Yes, home for the holidays is an enduring and powerful dream.

Consequently, it seems awkward—out of place even—when we read, in words we have cherished from childhood, that Jesus himself, the cause of all this, was *not* home for the holidays. Jesus was born in a strange town, his parents compelled to journey far from home by the edict of an alien ruler. Christ was born that first Christmas morning in a lonely cowshed, because times were so frantic under the occupying regime that there was no room in the inn. So I propose that we who *are*, for the most part, home for the holidays, we who have, at the very least, found room and welcome somewhere this Christmas Eve, take a moment to reflect on this

Christmas Eve

irony of history: that there was no place, no home for the holidays, no room at the inn, for the Son of God.

"No room, no room!" The cry of the innkeeper of Bethlehem. A familiar cry even now, two thousand years on. For we live in an era and in a society of no room. Perhaps it all goes back to those pioneer origins, that ever-expanding frontier out west, but this nation still seems to be obsessed with room, space, the exploration, the occupation, the control and command of physical space. Only glance at our two major spectator sports—first base, second base, third base, home!—ten yards, fifty yards, one hundred yards, touchdown! And all concerned with space, gaining space, guarding space, holding and controlling space. Take a look at our cities and highways where construction, expansion, the gobbling up of open land, seem never to halt. Take a look at our economy where the ownership of property (Isn't that why we call it *real* estate?) has been the key to financial security for generations. Why, even the new and purely virtual realms of the computer can only be visualized—it seems—in spatial terms, speaking of sites, domains, networks, chat rooms, home pages and the like.

In all of this, it seems to me, we can detect the presence and power of a dream, a wistful yet compelling dream that assures us that, if only we can control space, if we can somehow fill our space up, then we will finally be in control? And then, perhaps, that other, far more elusive element, time may come within our reach, and with it—who knows?—immortality. So we press on with our terminal pursuit of the trivial. And the heap rises, the clutter deepens, landfills explode, Goodwill stores expand and prosper. And at Christmas, in commemoration of one born with nothing, and who died owning only the robe on his back, we set out to buy ourselves everything.

And the result? No room! No room for solitude and quiet. Oh, there are still isolated spots where one can escape the machinery, the whine of the highway, the summons of the smartphone and the internet. But for how much longer? The din escalates. Communication seems almost total, but it has become almost impossible to hear, and there is nothing *to* hear, nothing worth

184

hearing anyway. Consider these words I found inscribed in a remote, eleventh-century abbey in southern France:

> *Le bruit ne fait pas de bien.*
> *Le bien ne fait pas de bruit.*
> Noise doesn't do any good.
> Good doesn't make any noise.

And the din is not just New York, Chicago, L.A., the U.S.A. The din has become the world. So that it won't be long before there is no room . . . no room for people. Unless the bombs, plagues, famine, what poet Robert Burns called, *man's inhumanity to man*, can clear a space.[1]

This holds true not only in society; in our personal lives too that innkeeper of Bethlehem strides back and forth muttering his "No room . . . no room!" Our days, hours, calendars are preoccupied—and that means *pre* occupied, booked solid in advance—sorry, no vacancies. "Must prepare for this. Must evaluate that. Must work now, exercise now, study now, play now, must run now." Everything with a purpose, a program, everything with a goal, and a schedule for getting there as rapidly as humanly possible.

Threatening as it may seem, perhaps we need to consider the possibility that, in the last account, we have no purpose? Or if we do, then that purpose is secondary to something far more important; and that is being: being alive, being human, being ourselves with others in the world. W. H. Auden is said to have remarked that art makes nothing happen. A review of a touring exhibit of works by the Dutch master Vermeer picked up on this observation:

> Vermeer's art makes nothing happen over and over again—the kind of stilled, breath-inheld, grace-infused and infusing "nothing" which is at the root of everything that matters.[2]

"Consider the lilies of the field, how they grow," said One for whom there was no room many centuries ago,

1. Barke, *Poems and Songs of Robert Burns*, 123.
2. Weschler, "Vermeer."

> . . . they neither toil nor spin; yet I tell you, even Solo-
> mon in all his glory was not arrayed like one of these
> (Matt 6:28–29).

Consider this world around us, within us. The utter useless-
ness, the splendid superfluity of snowflakes and sunflowers, of hol-
lyberries and hummingbirds, of poetry, music, wind, color, shape,
stars. Now if only *we* could have organized all this, if only Apple,
General Mills, Goldman Sachs, or the Pentagon could have been in
charge, things would have been so much tidier, so much more ef-
ficient, economical, practical, purposeful, productive. Thank God
they have not yet succeeded!

No room then, no room to be, no room for meaning, no
room for being, no room. So we carry on, hunting for the gift of
Christmas among the wrappings, the foil, the packaging material.
We go on filling ourselves with emptiness till we explode like so
many overinflated party balloons. We go on attempting to cover
everything, until everything conspires to cover us, death pulls its
final, unscheduled trick, and there is no room, no room for you,
for me, for us.

Yet Christ was born in Bethlehem, in a stable, of a woman
whom no one would believe was a virgin. Jesus was born *nevertheless*, in spite of all that, into a world which had no room. And
Christmas still does come, if you can find the room for it—room
for Christmas. It comes more often to mangers, Salvation Army
citadels, detention centers and refugee camps, than to Blooming-
dales or the Waldorf Astoria, but it still does come. A newborn
babe, the most perfectly purposeless gift in all creation, tells us
this. The Christ Child still does come, like a bundled basket left on
the chilly doorstep that we call the human heart.

One of the most magical moments of Christmas Eve for me,
as a pastor and leader of worship, happens during the ceremony
at the climax of the midnight service that we call "The Coming of
the Light." As the sanctuary is plunged into darkness, two young
acolytes come forward to light their tapers from the one remaining
source of light, the tall, majestic Christ candle. They then proceed,
as the choir softly leads into "Silent Night," to light the candles

on the communion table, the seven-branched candelabra, and the candles of clergy and choir, before processing down the center aisle, igniting the high candles at the head of every pew, and then the small, handheld one of the first person in each pew.

And as I watch, from my privileged vantage point in the chancel, the light is passed from hand to hand, the tiny candle flames progress toward the rear of the sanctuary, and faces slowly begin to appear out of the dark, a spreading, glowing, tapestry of human faces, almost haloed in the golden light. These are faces that, in the year almost gone, have known turmoil and trial, times of joy and sadness that I have often been privy to, as pastor and friend. And I say a silent prayer of thanks for all those radiant faces, for my calling to be their minister, and for a God who found room for Christmas, room for his son in stable and manger, room also for us, his vast, wandering, yet wonderful human family, to come back home, to be at home, to be at peace in his eternal presence.

So move over, wherever you find yourself this Christmas Eve. Make room, make ample room for Christmas: room for each other, room for yourself, room for God to be born in us, through us. Open up a few Advent windows—no, it's not too late—then leave them that way, wide open for the year that lies ahead. Rediscover the sacred blessing of hospitality in this season, hospitality not only to friends and relations—those who, like that Currier and Ives print, come bearing gifts. Let us, in this dark time of the revival of ancient fears, prejudice, and distrust, rediscover hospitality in our homes, our schedules, our bank accounts, our lives—hospitality above all to the stranger. For, as the Scriptures remind, in so doing we know not whom we will be welcoming. An old Celtic rune from the island of Iona, off the west coast of Scotland, sings thus:

> I saw a stranger yestreen.
> I put food in the eating place,
> drink in the drinking place,
> music in the music place . . .
> And in the sacred name of the Triune
> He blessed myself, my house,

Christmas Eve

> my cattle and my dear ones,
> and the lark said in her song,
> often, often, often
> goes the Christ in the stranger's guise.

So may this ancient blessing, this gift of hospitality, of the Christ Child in our midst, of room for Christmas and all it contains, be with us this Christmas Eve, and throughout this holy season.

∾

Gather us with angels, Lord, journey us with kings, hasten us with shepherds, humble us with ox and ass, and find room for us beside the manger, where your Son is born to bring us life, life forevermore. Amen.

Bethlehem Bound

(sudden summons)

You could see their sheep from the road,
way across on the hillside, grazing in the earliest half-light,
one of their company, with a couple of dogs,
left behind to keep things secure. The rest had passed us—
bedded down, as we were, by the side of the road—
not long ago, moving speedily, purposefully, almost silently,
but with a light of wild rejoicing in their eyes.

Back deeper in the night, with the creaking of saddles,
the complaining of beasts, three tall strangers, travel weary,
eyes fixed on the heavens, had also passed by
with much consultation and learned debate,
their path strangely lit by that low lying star in the east.

 And now, still just before dawn, we too are afoot,
not knowing, but hoping for something, not at all sure
just where we are headed, but convinced, nonetheless,
we must go. Bethlehem lies beyond.
A new day is dawning.
And see, at last, over the shadowing hills,
the first full rays of the sun!

Nativity

The songs and stories
all suggest a breathless hush,
that time stood sacred still
the moment that the child was born
and bedded, holy, in the manger.

But I suspect things tramped along
in much the way they ever did.
The watch was passed at Bethlehem's gate.
Torches were doused and hearth fires
banked with sod or dung till morning.
The innkeeper called time again,
and spread fresh-dampened sawdust on the floor.

The maid, emptying tavern-slops out back,
may just have paused a weary, hasty moment,
wondered at the more than lantern light
beneath the stable door,
the sudden, clamorous, urgency
of that infant's helpless cry.

Christmas Day

A Prayer for Christmas Day

Such an overflowing festival of gifts and giving, Lord.
Bright colored paper, fancy boxes, labels, bows and ribbons,
all the signs and symbols of generous affection
still litter the living room floor.
Their former contents, now revealed, sit heaped on chairs
and tables, waiting to be worn or read, played with
or tasted, used, enjoyed, appreciated.

There is an air of relaxed gratitude about the place,
a restful, mellow mood of thankfulness,
a sense that weeks and months of planning, scheming,
searching and researching have borne fruit,
been well worth the effort, and have ended in delight.
Old affection has been once again affirmed,
old hurts and grudges have been set aside,
new pledges made to try a little harder.

Grace has been said around the family table,
hands joined, the feast passed round from place to place,
and laughter shared, perhaps even a tear or two,
along with fond memories and thoughts
for all those missing,
absent from the circle, for whatever reason.

Take now these treasured moments, Father,
set them down as a grateful offering beside the crib,
let them remind us of your gift, your gift of life,
life itself in all its possibility and promise,
life displayed, poured out for us within a newborn child.

Christmas Day

Show us again how to receive, O God,
to receive this life you give, and live it freely in return.
As you have given us yourself—Divinity traced in human form—
so teach us to return the gift,
to open up these frail and fallible human lives
and let your divine life flow through them.

Take all of this day's gratitude now, and turn it into action,
into good, old-fashioned deeds of love and mercy,
into plans and programs for community and justice,
into ways of building that "peace on earth, goodwill to all"
of which your angels sang so long ago.

Accept our thanks, Lord God,
for each and every gift this Christmas Day,
and through the blessing of the manger child
transform them into life,
that life for others that he lived among us,
died to show us the way,
and rose again to vindicate forever.
Amen.

A Word for Feeble Knees

Strengthen the weak hands, and make firm the feeble knees. Say to those who are of a fearful heart, "Be strong, fear not!"

—Isaiah 35:3-4

Have you felt it yet? Did it, perhaps, surprise you as you heard your first carol on the radio, or fixed the final decoration onto this year's tree? Did it creep up on you with the Christmas mail, or even—perish the thought—in the Christmas mall? The Christmas spirit is what I'm thinking of, that difficult to define, yet quite definite sensation that tells you that it's here again, or rather *you're* here again, back in that splendid realm of anticipation and surprise, secrets and suspense, that has touched and warmed the chill midwinter of your life since your earliest memories began. Have you felt it yet?

Maybe that's why you are taking the time to read these words just now, right in the midst of this day of celebration. Might it just be that, in all the fuss and bother of getting ready: all the bargain hunting, standing in check-out line after check-out line (I heard someone say that anyone who thinks Christmas doesn't last all year long must not have a credit card) might it be that, between telephone calls and travel arrangements, between sending out invitations and accepting them, between buying, baking and budgeting, between all these essential activities of the season, there has not been time for getting into the Christmas spirit? And so now, at the very last minute, even later than the eleventh hour, on Christmas Day itself, in these readings, poems, and prayers, you are hoping to find, or perhaps be found by, that magic we still call "the spirit of Christmas."

The trouble is that after all that other stuff, that frenzy of schedules and deadlines, you are hardly in any shape for a magical moment of any kind whatsoever. It's too late in the day already, and your back aches, your feet are sore, your eyes are red, and what you really need is an armchair, a hot and spicy drink, and a backrub. Maybe this is just a waste of time after all. "Bah . . . Humbug!" And then the Scripture reading, when you finally find it, starts out by addressing those who have weak hands and feeble knees. "Good grief!" You murmur, "Could this writer be talking about me?"

This Christmas story, this announcement that Isaiah foresaw centuries before it came to pass, is addressed precisely to the likes of you and me in all our aching, rushing-to-get-there-on-time weariness. Indeed, if we had actually set out to prepare ourselves throughout these weeks of Advent for the hearing of today's message we could not have done a more effective job. Listen to it again:

> Strengthen the weak hands, and make firm the feeble knees. Say to those who are of a fearful heart, "Be strong, fear not!"

Now we *do* know what that feels like. "Good grief, I think he *is* talking to me!"

Consider, for a moment, those to whom this message came in the first place, those to whom the holy child was revealed. A poor, bewildered carpenter and his young bride far from home, a group of cold and hungry shepherds working the night shift, a worn-out, over-booked innkeeper, and a trio of travel-weary, wise, but definitely elderly men, hardly the most promising, the most vigorous, the most confidence inspiring collection of witnesses. And throughout this holy infant's life it was with the feeble and the weak, the ailing, the hurting and the broken ones, he chose to spend his time. He was crucified there too, still among them at the end. So if you feel a little weary, just a bit breathless at the manger, then take heart; because this message is for you; it is precisely for you.

It speaks above all else to the poor and homeless, the hungry, oppressed and friendless of our world, and we must never let ourselves forget that, or our celebrations will be false as Santa's whiskers. But it speaks, God speaks this very day, to all those who are burdened, or in any way heavy-laden, whether with regrets for the past, heartache here in the present, forebodings for the future. And God says to us, to all of us:

> Be strong, fear not, for I am with you, I am for you and
> I will never let you go. Here is my son to prove it to you.

"What's the catch, then?"—you may ask, as a typical, skeptical, consumer of today—"What about the fine print, the hidden costs, all those items that I must give up, set aside, or take on, in order to receive this gift, this grace, this divine comfort and assurance?"

We're always looking for the catch in Christmas, always wary, fearful of what God really has in mind, what God will ask of us in return. But suppose God was truly, and supremely, and above all else, the great Giver, just that, the great Giver. (Didn't you ever wonder why Christmas was all about giving? It wasn't thought up by Sears, you realize, or even Macy's.) Just suppose that God, who devised this whole thing, this entire universe, in the first place, knew all along what we have only guessed at thus far; that giving is really much more fun than getting; that nothing in all creation can quite match the joy of seeing someone unwrap a gift that you have selected with your deepest and most careful love.

Now suppose that's what God is actually like, what God and life itself—reality in fact—are really all about, so that in giving us his Son, sending us that greatest gift there ever was or will be, God got such a charge, such sheer delight out of the whole thing that the entire creation laughed with him and rang with joy. That's what the carols have long been telling us surely. Don't you hear them?

> O come, all ye faithful, *joyful* and triumphant . . .
> *Joyful,* all ye nations, rise, Join the triumph of the skies . . .
> Good Christian Friends, *rejoice*, with heart, and soul, and
> voice . . .
> *Joy* to the world, the Lord is come . . .

Why do we Christians, particularly—I suspect—we Protestants, direct descendants of the Puritans, always have to see Christmas as God's last resort, the final, grudging, super-sacrificial act of a deity who had tried everything else—Moses and the Law, the prophets, and so forth—and failed? Is there not a real sense in which that night in Bethlehem was the culmination of the cosmos, the very apex, the climax of creation, the moment when the love of God (which clearly had been there from the beginning) took on its highest, truest, fullest form, and came among us to be known, touched and shared, to be loved and then lived out, by every one of us? And so God laughed for joy on that first Christmas Eve, and all the rejoicing hosts of heaven joined in.

So where does that leave us, with our weak hands, feeble knees and fearful hearts? If God has done all this for us out of sheer amazing, outrageous grace, what is there left for us to do? There is a lovely ancient tale they tell about those shepherds around Bethlehem, how they loved to sit debating in the long night watches out on the Judean hills. One night toward dawn their spiritual guide, an older shepherd, posed them a probing question. "How can we know when the night has ended and the day has begun?"

"Could it be . . . ," one of the young ones blurted out eagerly, "might we know the night is ended when we can look out to the flock and distinguish between the sheepdog and the sheep?"

"That is a good answer," said the teacher, "but not the answer I would give."

After a long silence another raised his voice, "Perhaps we know daylight has begun when we can look at the trees around us and distinguish the olive leaf from the fig."

Again the teacher shook his head. "A fine answer, but not the one I seek."

At last they begged their teacher to share the answer he had in mind. He looked at each of them intently for a moment and then he said, "When you look into the eyes of a human being and see a sister or a brother, you know that it is morning. If you cannot see a sister or brother, then you will know it is still night."

This is a day, an entire season, of wondrous joy, of radiant hope, of newborn yet eternal love. Therefore:

Strengthen the weak hands,
and make firm those feeble knees.

Discover in yourself, in your neighbor, in the outcast stranger and the fearful friend that very Christmas spirit you began today in search of. Then go forth to share God's glorious laughter, as you find the meaning of your life newborn in living love and giving love away; and doing this, yes doing it all, with joy.

∼

Bless us now, Lord God, with the true delight, the age-old joy of Christmas, and may that joy, through us, show grace to all in need, bring blessing to everyone we meet. Amen.

The Silent Seers

Of all the witnesses around that holy manger
perhaps it was the animals saw best what lay ahead
for they had paced the aching roads,
slept in the wet and hungry fields,
known the sharp sting of sticks and thorns and curses,
endured the constant bruise of burdens not their own
the tendency of men to use and then discard
rather than meet and pay the debt of gratitude.
For them the future also held the knacker's rope,
the flayer's blade, the tearing of their bodies
for the sparing of a race.
In the shadows of that stable
might it be his warmest welcome
lay within their quiet, comprehending gaze?

Twelve Days of Christmas

THE MORNING AFTER

Boxing Day is what we called it back in England,
day after Christmas Day, when all those who delivered
to the door, the tradesmen, clattering milkman, postman,
paperboy, grocer's boy, driver of the baker's van
which smelled so heavenly steaming rich of hot new bread,
fresh scones and teacakes, mixed with all the warm
and tangy odors of the patient steady horse, harnessed in front
and munching on its nose bag, there was the butcher's boy
on a bicycle, his apron blue and white and flecked with spots
of blood, bearing along a whiff of the sawdust floor,
the hanging sides of beef and pork, the suet
and the sausages as he delivered cool and yielding
brown-wrapped parcels at the kitchen door,
all these received their Christmas Box, which must,
in Dickens' time, have been a veritable box, a carton filled
with Xmas Cheer of sundry sorts, but, by my early youth,
this all had settled for a sixpence or a shilling, if you were
really lucky maybe half-a-crown. Whatever, it spread
the generous season out at least another day, postponed
that dreary moment when you fall back into winter,
wondering if you will ever make it through till spring.

Another favorite for Boxing Day was to attend
the pantomime, or "Panto," as it everywhere was known.
Boxing Day was always best for that, although the show
continued on till well after the holidays had ended.
They would take a fairy tale or nursery rhyme,
Puss in Boots, Old Mother Hubbard—Dick Whittington

I liked best—and flesh it out into a full-length show
with folk dressed up as animals,
men playing crotchety old dames,
young buxom women cast as handsome lads
and lots of slapping feathered hats on flashing thighs,
and music, trapdoors, vulgar jokes and pratfalls,
sometimes even fairies flying out across the audience,
of which the first five rows formed "The Enchanted Forest,"
flying on thin invisible wires you could almost—hardly—see
if you half closed your eyes. Well, such a day!

I wonder nowadays just what the Christ Child
would have made of Boxing Day back then.
Would he pour scorn and judgment over all those
patronizing little gifts, symbols of an unequal social order?
Might he denounce the bawdy commonness, the tawdry
tinsel glitter of the Panto and its creaking old performers?
But then, again, perhaps the Child would laugh and cry
and cheer, and clap his hot and sticky hands with glee
just like we did as evil-hearted villains were defeated,
maidens saved, and heroes at last vindicated.
Might he even clasp a sixpence to himself and run
back home to share it, conscious only of the gift
which made at least one further day shine bright
with heaven's brimming generosity?

Merry Christmas! Third and Final Notice.

*Then, opening their treasures, they offered him gifts, gold and
frankincense and myrrh.*

—Matthew 2:11

It all came back while sorting through the Christmas mail recently, as I realized that, since moving into a retirement community,
we had been missing at least one customary piece, one unfailingly
regular item among our annual accumulation of season's greetings.
I'm thinking of that colorful, yet quite empty envelope from our
friendly neighborhood trash collectors. All their names would be
on it—handwritten, of course, just like old pals—along with pictures of scarlet poinsettias. And the message was unmistakeably
clear. "It's that time of year again. Tis the season to be generous."
All of which reminded me of just such an envelope, received several Christmases before, when we lived in New York City. It came
from those jolly sanitation folks, and it too bore cheery seasons
greetings. But then, down in the lower right-hand corner, it also
bore these somewhat menacing, additional words: Third, and *Final* Notice!

Merry Christmas, then, "Third and *Final* Notice!" And, as
The Day Itself is finally upon us, that's just the way it seems to be
so much of the time. An appropriate scriptural text to accompany
such a message might be found in those words about the magi
appearing at the beginning of today's meditation:

Then, opening their treasures, they offered him gifts . . .

because it's those gifts I want to focus upon, those gifts and what our giving—all this present seeking, present buying, wrapping, unwrapping and returning business—does to Christmas. Who is there, after all, who has not stopped to ponder whether the hustle and bustle—particularly the hustle—of these past few weeks has finally transformed this sacred festival into one vast commercial grab bag? When those three wise men offered the very first Christmas gifts at the manger did they have any idea of the sheer exhaustion, the utter madness, not to mention the crushing financial overload, they were wishing upon future generations? Giving, then, holiday giving, is it blessing or bane, the heart or the hurt of Christmas?

I think everyone might agree at the outset that the basic idea is an excellent one. What more lovely way to commemorate God's gift of his Son to us than by giving symbols of *our* love to those we hold dear? The trouble is, like so many other basically excellent ideas, this giving has a tendency to get out of control. The result is that all too often we end up giving gifts not out of love, but out of obligation . . . Third and *Final* Notice! . . . gifts, in other words, not to make a person happy, but to cancel out a debt, or even worse, to create a debt on someone else's ledger. There develops, all too often, a scarce-concealed competitiveness, a finely calibrated calculation to determine the precise equivalent, or as close as possible to it, of whatever it was that we received (from whomever it was) last year. And in the background lurks that ultimate reassurance that, if they don't like it, it can always be returned. Now I realize it does make a lot of practical sense to return or exchange gifts you don't want or need. Yet doesn't something happen to the meaning of a gift, the way it is chosen, the way it is received, when you have to take care how you unwrap it in case you will need to claim a refund? And that is not even to mention the more recent holiday tradition that people euphemistically call "*re*-gifting."

This whole question about giving and generosity, not only at Christmas, raises serious issues for today's church. I've been reading a lot lately about a whole category of reputedly successful churches—*megachurches* they are called—designed to cater to the younger generation, those millennials and their new, developing families. Part of their secret, it is reported, is that they make few demands, seek little in the way of commitment, always send people away with a handshake and a smile, and never, ever ask for money. Could *that* be why so many of our more mainstream congregations fail to make their pledge goals in these difficult economic times? Their mistake is in the asking!

A letter I received from an inquirer phrased the question thus:

> Every day at the dinner table my father included in his blessing the phrase, "Make us ever mindful of the needs of others." My problem is figuring how we can ever think of our own needs if we are *ever* mindful of others. Plus, if we do think of ourselves, how do we avoid feeling guilty?

It *is* a bit of a monster, that brief but bothersome prayer. I usually manage to get it backwards so that it comes out, "Ever needful of the minds of others," which is, when you stop to think about it, not too bad a description of our human condition. But what about this whole business of giving, giving at Christmas, giving to the church, giving to help others, giving to those less fortunate than ourselves?

It seems to me we make our big mistake in focusing on what to give, rather than how to give and why. The Scriptures know only one motivation for giving, that of gratitude, and not obligation. And they recognize only one way to give, not guiltily, but joyfully! I'll never forget preaching at the Presbyterian Church of the Resurrection in downtown Accra, in Ghana, West Africa. When the presiding minister announced the offering and I reached for my wallet, the enormously dignified elder in full tribal dress, seated beside me on the podium, leaned across and murmured: "This is the *first* offering." I speedily became grateful for that warning, since there were three more offerings before I got up to preach. And on each occasion those giving people came parading down the center aisle, singing a joyful hymn, clapping their hands and swaying, and tossing their gifts into two huge woven baskets at the foot of the chancel steps. Their giving was a genuine celebration, a celebration of God's vast generosity to them, and of their privilege in returning some of these gifts to God. How is it that we so often miss out on the sheer joy, the genuine exhilaration of generous giving?

As for finding the perfect gift: for all our comparison shopping, all our scanning of the ads and catalogues, and, more and more today, the internet, we will never find it. Because the perfect gift is yourself—your own self—your time, your attention, your affection, your life. And that is what God gave, still gives, at Christmastime.

In an e-mail communication a few years ago our third daughter, Nicola, was trying to give her family here at home some sense of what she was involved in, in her work for UNICEF. "Approximately fifteen-thousand children work, live and sleep on the streets of Accra," she wrote:

> . . . many of them are young girls and the numbers are growing. One of these girls is Sadia, a *Kayayoo*, or market load carrier, who works all day carrying huge loads on her young head. She gets cheated a lot, and she gets sick. She is twelve years old. And then there is Adiatu who washes dishes at the roadside from morning into the night. Adiatu earns about fifty cents a day. She is eleven years old and cannot go to school. She came to Accra with her mother a year ago to make some survival money and then go back to their village. Her mother is aged twenty-six and a load carrier. They live with Sadia and some eighty other women and girls on a narrow verandah behind some government buildings. In the rainy season everyone sleeps standing up because the place is awash. There is piped water, but no latrines. They have to use the gutter or the ground. Sadia and Adiatu and the rest are frequently threatened with eviction. There is no security here, or anywhere else in Accra. They are at the mercy of office workers and unscrupulous night-watchmen. The authorities regard them as a nuisance, to be moved on, to be harrassed, to be abused. These are just a few of the girls who live, work, and sleep on the streets of Accra, some of them as young as seven or eight. They have the same aspirations and dreams as any other girls. They could be your daughters, your sisters, yourselves.

Somehow a letter like that puts *our* needs, *our* problems concerning giving into another context. It sets one enormous question mark against our anxious dithering about whether to choose the green necktie or the red one, or just take both.

A highlight of winter weekends for many people—apart from the operas themselves—is the intermission quiz on the weekly Metropolitan Opera broadcasts. I was listening in, one Advent Saturday, and stumbled upon an insight into this ongoing concern over giving. The questions on that particular day involved miracles in opera, and the contestants were asked to recall an opera in which a lame shepherd boy suddenly was able to walk, which they swiftly identified as Gian Carlo Menotti's *Amahl and the Night Visitors*. But the experts were stymied on the circumstances, the actual situation within the plot of the opera, in which that miracle took place. The genial host filled in the gap, telling how, when the cripple-boy Amahl sees the gifts that his night visitors, the three kings, are bearing to the newborn Prince of Peace, he yearns to share in their generous acts. So he offers them the only thing he has to give, his one solitary possession, his crutch, to carry to the infant Jesus. And as he holds out that bent and battered crutch, Amahl takes first one stumbling step, then another, two and then three, and finally begins to run and even dance. That sophisticated radio host/opera buff went on to confess that that scene invariably brings tears to his eyes—as it does to mine—and I began to wonder what, in that magical moment, has the power to speak so tenderly to the heart. And there it was, the secret of true giving, and also true healing, the one miraculous thing that can make all our Christmases truly rich, rich with the wonder of God's presence.

Healing, reconciliation, sheer delight, the ability to dance and sing, and set out upon adventure—all of these arise out of the utterly simple, utterly spontaneous ability to give, to give oneself, to take what one has, and lives by, and holds onto, and hold it out in selfless, joyful love toward another person. This is the genius of what Menotti tells us, that when we see the Christ child, the life he offers us is discovered and received just when we least expect it, just as we thought we were giving it away.

> For those who would save their life will lose it, and those
> who lose their life for my sake will find it . . .

Merry Christmas, then . . . Third and *Final* Notice! For there *is* a note of warning, a nagging little footnote scribbled down there near the bottom, the suggestion, at least, of an impending deadline attached to all of our Christmas giving and receiving. There are just so many Christmases allotted to each lifetime, only a certain number of opportunities to learn this delicate art of giving and receiving. The Christ whose return we pray for in this season will not come back again as a harmless little child. If we are to believe the Scripture, the next time it will be as judge, as the ulltimate one who judges you and me.

We have been granted a reprieve, another year, another season of lights on trees and old familiar songs across the frost-sharpened air, another time for distant greetings in the mail and family reunions, another opportunity to slow down and watch the snowflakes fall, the geese head south, the long slow fading of winter afternoons, the settling of embers in the fireplace, the flickering of candle-flame reflected in the eyes of those we cherish. Now, while there is still time, we must find, in all of these, a way to give, to give ourselves, to abandon all that frantic running after stuff and style, sensation and success, and rediscover love, the one gift we can own only as we freely give it away.

We have been given another Christmas. Let us give back to it ourselves, our hopes and fears, enmities and affections, our timid, yet still yearning hearts, that in the giving, in the openness and trust, in the new beginnings that all this can open up, we might discover, as old Ebenezer Scrooge did, awakening after his long night of wrestling with ominous visions to the joy of that legendary London Christmas morning long ago:

> No fog, no mist, clear, bright, jovial, stirring, cold; piping
> hot the blood to dance to; Golden sunlight; heavenly sky;
> sweet fresh air; merry bells; Oh, glorious. Glorious!

And so we might discover with Scrooge that Christmas is not past, not even yet fully present, but is about to begin, just waiting for you and me, waiting for us to give ourselves, to lose ourselves, to find ourselves reborn beside the manger.

∾

Take, now, this holy moment, this consecrated instant of our time, and bless it with the presence of eternity. Make it radiant with your glory, vibrant with the promise of new life found in the Babe of Bethlehem. Amen.

Don't Stop Me ...

if you've heard this one before.
It all begins, you see,
with an amazed young virgin wondering by the well,
then proceeds, past puzzled Joseph, to a manger
in a cattle stall. Some shepherds get involved,
and three venerable Magi from the east
led by a star. A narrow escape
is followed by the usual brutalities.
And then . . .

You know the rest, of course.
But in this chill and wintered season
when depth draws near, despite the merchandizing
and the malls, to hear it all once more in song,
and speech, and simple celebration,
can bring light to darkness, trust beyond all fear,
and a gentle way to walk, at least until you hear
this time-worn, secret-splendid tale
for yet another year.

INCARNATING

Becoming
putting on
clothing oneself
assuming flesh
bearing the bone-and-blood
mortality that bears us all
through what we call
for better or for worse
this life
how did he do it?

Was it like
climbing
clumsy
into
heavy, clanking armor
slipping on
a skin-tight wet suit
taking on oneself a body-cast
of stiff unyielding clay?

Or
was there more of
taking off
a shedding
of the iridescent skin
of fair eternity
a love-filled
laying to one side
of glory, majesty, and power
before the naked plunge into the
depths to seek a treasure long encrusted
by the sifting sands of night?

Christmas Haiku

Joseph's Wish

Rest, my Mary, rest.
Your child sleeps sound beside you,
all creation blessed.

Mary's Moment

Blue and gold align
purity breathless awaits
trembling stillness.

Hearth

Hopeful stockings hang suspended
expecting to be filled
and emptied.

Warning

White Christmas dreaming songs
will surely lead to shovels,
salt, sore backs.

The Midwife of Bethlehem

Why do we make such a fuss,
after all, about birth?
Surely we know what is happening,
bound to happen sooner or later,
disease, drink, cold blind accident,
too little food, too many brains,
the usual and always final event
gets them all, get us all, in the end.

So why, in the name of heaven,
are all these idiot shepherds here,
far from their fold, fouling the air
and the streets with their rancid flocks?
And these dark, distinguished strangers,
confused, spent with much travel,
mumbling together of stars, gold, other gifts?

Indeed, you'd think even the dumb beasts
in their stalls had been told something
and were waiting, reverent somehow,
at this hasty, un-provided birth.

Yet, when all is said and done,
there was something about that young mother,
trusting, calm, confident for a first timer.
And the baby, so bold, aware already . . .
Why, I do believe the child is smiling,
looking right over here, bless my soul, at me.

Get out of my way, sheep,
while I kneel a moment, rest my weary legs
before I leave, and view this newest infant
that my red old hand has slapped
from death to free and gasping life
this odd, and almost holy night.

FAMILY VALUES

This holiest of families was, by all accounts,
a quite irregular affair, the father far too old
for such a bride, the teenage mother's pregnancy
ill-timed, to say the least, and, perhaps, also ill-fathered.
Or so the gossip went.

As for the child, brought forth
in un-provided haste and far from home and kin,
laid bundled in a feeding trough for cattle; all kinds
of odd, unsavory characters, vagabonds, transient aliens,
and wanderers are said to have sought out his birth,
just the sort who ought to be reported
to the appropriate authorities.

The father disappears as the tale unfolds
after a brief incident of apparent child neglect
when the boy was only twelve years old;
while the mother and various other siblings
are publicly rebuked and then disowned.

Hardly, in other words, a family unit to sing songs about,
or to portray upon the mantel of one's hearth;
hardly the kind of folks one would wish
to welcome for the holidays.

HEROD'S DREAM

Fish, there were,
great schooling shoals,
and one who strolled among their ripples
tall as a shepherd with his flocks.

Temple jars
tipped over scattered tables,
trickled blood,
—or was it wine?—
across a mellow face
that laughed so long and fine
he washed the slopes of Olive Mountain
with his tears.

There limped a donkey
ringed with dusty cheers
beneath a harlequin
who palmed my fearful city as his own.
While at his broken heels
vast festal meals were spread
for royal guests and vagabonds
all supping simple bread with ruby vintage.

Drunken star-songs
rolled along bright heavens
to a stable brimmed
with sheep-fold men and magi.

Those murmuring strangers,
once again,
casting their purple
calculations on the night.

I thought I saw a gallows cross
become a throne, high, lifted up
through rending grave clothes
and a splintered stone.
Then, as it ended,
a whole regiment of children,
infants really, danced me from my palace,
piping through the gaping lips of bloody Sheol.

This dream demands immediate interpretation.
Send for my guards!

The Foolishness of Love

Behold a young woman shall conceive and bear a son, and shall call his name Immanuel.

—ISAIAH 7:14

To be completely honest, there are many foolish things about this Bible. Most obviously there are the talking animals, seas that dry up overnight, fortified city walls that come tumbling down at the blast of a trumpet, free food that falls from heaven every evening, or is delivered fresh each day by flocks of ravens, that reluctant prophet swallowed by a whale, then thrown up alive three days later on the beach. Then there are all those idyllic prophecies, pledges and promises of universal justice and peace—leopards and lambs taking a nap together and the like—a future time when folk will lay aside their weapons and learn to live together in harmony. Well, it's been close to 3000 years now and what happened to all that harmony?

But, of all these absurdities, surely the most ludicrous is this whole business of *Immanuel*—God with us, this belief that the Almighty Creator, the Alpha and Omega—beginning and end of everything that is, ever has been, ever will be—that such a divine being should "come down and join us." That means not simply visit us, drop in on his lesser creation seeking momentary amusement as those Greek deities used to do from time to time, but should actually join us, within the span of one human life, be born and toddle as a child, grow through the turmoil years of adolescence, learn love and rejection, laughter and pain at firsthand, sense the greening lilt of springtime, the burning summer sun, the bitter chill of winter, taste wine and bread and song across the lips, receive the cruel sting of whips and nails into his fragile flesh. What a curious belief! Or, to be unkind, but ruthlessly honest: what a load of foolishness!

Yet is it really all that curious? Someone has noted that in the year 1809, midway between the historic battles of Trafalgar and Waterloo, when the entire world's attention was riveted on the actions, plans and prospects of one man, the Emperor Napoleon, a group of babies were being born into this world. There was Gladstone, the future British leader, reformer, and Prime Minister; there was Alfred Tennyson, the future poet laureate; here in the U.S. there were Oliver Wendell Holmes and out in the hills of Kentucky a certain Abraham Lincoln. On the European continent there was born in that same year a child called Frederick Chopin and another Felix Mendelssohn. All that anyone thought about in 1809 was battles, campaigns, politics, global strategy. But after now 200 years, which do you think, in the long run, made more of a historic difference, those battles or those babies?

I realize it doesn't make sense; I realize that logic would easily refute this proposition that the Lord of all creation, the One who holds this vast universe in being, should, at the same time, be fully present in one human life here on earth. It just does not compute! But since when did logic even begin to describe with any adequacy the most vital, crucial things of your life and mine—our loves, our fears, the hopes, anxieties, dreams and dreads that motivate or dominate our days?

And if this doesn't make sense, if love, the love of God poured into one radiant, resonant, human life seems utter nonsense, then consider the alternatives. For example, those beer commercials on TV that keep telling us, "It doesn't get any better than this." All those lithe young bodies, skiing the mountains, shooting the rapids, scaling dizzying rock faces, camping under the stars, and then popping open their foaming cans of all that represents the good life—money, health, good looks, good times, success. "It doesn't get any better than this?" Well, if that's the case, if it truly does not get any better, and that's the best we can hope for, then you can count me out. It's just not enough. It never *has* been enough. And I suspect that's why many of us were crowding into churches just a few days ago looking for something different.

A closing story: a story about a baby and about foolishness, yet a story that is true, true to life, perhaps even eternal life. During her second pregnancy Karen's three-year-old son, Michael, formed a tight bond with his unborn sister by singing to her every night, his head pressed close against his mother's side. At delivery there were complications, and the little girl was born struggling to survive. After several difficult, seemingly endless days, the neonatologist began to prepare Karen and her husband for the worst. Outside the ICU stood Michael, anxious, asking, as he had done every day, to see his new sister. Finally, when all hope seemed lost, Karen dressed the little boy in oversized scrubs and led him in, defying the protests of some of the staff. What foolishness! How utterly unwise! What damage might this do to the child? Michael went over to the bassinette, pressed his face close as he could, and sang:

> You are my sunshine, my only sunshine.
> You make me happy, when skies are gray.
> You'll never know dear how much I love you.
> Please don't take my sunshine away.

They called it "Michael's miracle." Next day, instead of planning a funeral, Karen and her husband took Michael's sister home. She had responded, almost immediately, to her brother's well-known voice, and she was restored to life.

This foolish God of ours is out to sing *us* back to life in this season of Christ's birth. In the well-loved music of the carols, in moments of holy, precious silence, in the fragrance of evergreens, in the gentle light of candles, God is singing to us if we will listen, singing a song that we learned before we were born. It is a song of hope, a song of trust, a song of foolish, yet undying love.

We can catch it, even now, in the voices of neighbors, in the voices of the homeless on our streets, in the voices of children, all those innocents whose days are still threatened by the savage swords of power, politics, and privilege. We can hear it in the voices of all those who need our love, yet, out of their need, can also feed our love and help it grow. So listen now for the voice of God, our foolish, flagrant, loving, and forever forgiving God, and let God sing us back to life again.

～

Amid all the deafening noise of these days, Lord, the sounds of radio and telephone, of television and tablet, the din from the streets and highways, the clamor of our own inner voices, let us hear your enduring, gracious song. And may it lead us in the quiet ways of truth and peace. Amen.

New Year's Day

A River Runs Through Us

For a thousand years in thy sight, are but as yesterday when it is past,
or as a watch in the night.

—Psalm 90:4

You observe days and months and seasons and years! I am afraid I
have labored over you in vain.

—Galatians 4:10–11

No matter how frequently the scientists, the physicists and astronomers tell us nowadays that it is all finally an illusion, time, and the passage of time, constitute one of the most endur- ing enigmas of human existence. As the great Augustine once remarked, time is something we think more about, talk more about, yet understand less about, than almost anything else in all creation. In our own era, Rabbi Abraham Heschel has noted that time is the only dimension of our living that is completely beyond our control. "We may succeed in conquering space . . ." Heschel writes, "but time remains immune to our power."[1]

What about time, then, on this day when we have to replace our calendars and diaries, this day we call *New Years*? What is the meaning of this element, this controlling, yet uncontrollable environment we inhabit, this profound mystery we are all of us immersed in, whether we like it or not? It can seem so regular, so rigid, so unyielding, most of the time, ticking away, counting off our allotted span of hours, days and years on all those high-tech,

1. Heschel, *The Insecurity of Freedom*, 79.

digital devices that surround us nowadays. Time can appear to be so regular. Yet this same phenomenon, in other settings, can be experienced in such flexible and fluid, elastic ways that certain moments, for example over these holidays just past, may seem to have been stretched, expanded almost into hours, while other hours, even days, flash past and are gone before we notice them. What is this thing called time? How can we *begin* to describe it, to define it, let alone comprehend it?

It dawned on me some years ago that when we think about time we do so on at least two different levels: levels that I call Micro-time and Macro-time. The first of these is the ordinary, everyday level on which we construct our calendars and date books, allotting time for this and for that, seeking time for new commitments, yearning for free time to catch up on time, complaining because there never seems to be enough of it. Micro-time I call this, the close-up, detailed view of the passing moments that make up our daily living. It was of such a view that the Roman poet and playwright Plautus wrote:

> The gods confound the man . . . who set up a sundial to
> cut and hack my days wretchedly into small portions.[2]

Then there is Macro-time, that wider, more encompassing, all embracing view that takes in not only the trees, but the forest as well, that looks beyond the daily details, to the years, decades, lifetimes even. This second level is one we tend to visit, we prefer to visit, far less often, but also one that touches us, nudges us, forces its way into our consciousness with unusual insistence, uncomfortable persistence at this time of year. It caught me just a few weeks ago as I staggered up from our storage unit carrying several large and dusty boxes full of Christmas decorations and suddenly thought, "Good grief, I only put these down here two or three months ago. It surely can't be that time again already." Then along comes New Year—Hogmanay, as we call it in Scotland—and, despite all attempts with parties, bottles, noise-makers and balloons, there are few who can evade that, at least momentary, haunting,

2. http://www.laphamsquarterly.org/time/hacked-days.

glimpse of the years slipping by like so much sand, drifting, sifting through our fingers into nothingness. "Time, like an ever-rolling stream . . ." runs that majestic hymn we sing at funerals and other solemn occasions:

> Time like an ever-rolling stream
> Bears all its sons (and daughters too) away.
> They fly forgotten as a dream
> Dies at the opening day.

Yes, a river runs through us; and that river's name is Time; and it carries us along with it; it bears us all away.

It was not ever thus. It has not always been with us, this brooding sense of Macro-time, but tends to come on—at least in my experience—ever more strongly, more urgently with the passing of the years. Someone has remarked:

> Life can be pretty grim when you reach eighty;
> especially if there's a police car coming up behind.

Isn't Macro-time just a bit like that, like some cosmic patrol car with flashing lights and wailing siren, drawing ever closer in the rearview mirror?

> But at my back I alwaies hear
> Time's winged chariot hurrying near.
> And yonder all before us lie
> Desarts of vast Eternitie.

wrote Andrew Marvell centuries ago, in his lines to his "coy mistress."

Yet, to repeat, it was not ever so. Most of us, I suspect, retain somewhere from childhood the memory of one magical summer, a gloriously spacious time when sunlit days of forest, lake and shore, picnics and blue skies, stretched on and on and never seemed to end. What was it that we knew back then and seem to have lost forever? Was it merely some childish fancy, an echo of an innocence that never really was? Or might this have been a part, at least, an aspect of what Jesus meant when he told us, if we would enter the kingdom of Heaven, to become again like little children?

The secret of those golden days of childhood lay in this, the absence of fear, the absence of the fear of death. Death is what transforms our sense of time into a threat and no longer a blessing. Death is what constricts our days, pursues us down the narrowing corridors of the years, and then awaits us at the end. The Epistle to the Hebrews describes ". . . all those who through fear of death were subject to lifelong bondage" (Heb 2:15). While Sir Walter Raleigh, on the eve of his execution, wrote poignant words, later found on the flyleaf of his Bible:

> Even such is time, which takes in trust
> Our youth, our joys, and all we have,
> And pays us but with age and dust;
> Who in the dark and silent grave
> When we have wandered all our ways
> Shuts up the story of our days.[3]

So it is that the farther down the road we travel, the closer we draw to that final destination, the more we find ourselves looking, not forward anymore, but backward, cherishing memories more than hopes, past achievements more than future plans and dreams. Even those snapshots we took over these past holidays suggest this truth; for in them are we not trying to stop the clock, freeze one blessed moment, seize at least one smile and hold it safe forever? Yes, a river runs through us; and that flowing river's name is *time*.

Is there a way to do more than this, more than dread the dates, anniversaries, birthdays, the steady inexorable turning of the pages of the calendar? Paul believed there was. This was what infuriated him about those Galatian Christians to whom he wrote in the words of our text:

> You observe days and months and seasons and years! I
> am afraid I have labored over you in vain..

3. In Hayward, *The Penguin Book*, 38.

For Paul, as for so many of our Christian forbears, even some today who still face peril and death for the faith, this threat of death was no longer a valid one. The passing years to him were not mere milestones on life's journey to the tomb; all had been transformed, turned upside down by one colossal fact, the central fact, indeed, of our faith, the fact of Jesus Christ. No longer cherishing, or clinging to the past, Paul writes to the believers at Philippi:

> ... forgetting what lies behind and straining forward to what lies ahead, I press on toward the goal for the prize of the upward call of God [he's writing about death, here] in Christ Jesus (Phil 3:13–14).

What a view of life and death, from a condemned man on death row in a Roman prison! Not peering wistfully backward to the glory days now gone, but leaning forward, ready, even eager to launch out, to know what secrets are about to be unveiled by this God who has shown himself so decisively, so conclusively in Jesus Christ our Savior. With such a God as this in charge of time what then is left to fear? "If God be for us," Paul writes in Romans 8:31, "who can be against us?" And again:

> O death, where is thy victory?
> O death, where is thy sting?
> The sting of death is sin, and the power of sin is the law.
> But thanks be to God, who gives us the victory through our Lord Jesus Christ (1 Cor 15:55–57).

And yet again:

> For I am sure that neither death, nor life, nor angels, nor principalities, nor things present, nor things to come, nor powers, nor height, nor depth, nor anything else in all creation, will be able to separate us from the love of God, in Christ Jesus our Lord. (Romans 8:38–39).

Could it, might it even be, that the glory of our faith holds out to us again precisely what we thought we had lost, forfeited, given up forever: that enduring childhood vision of the endless, fearless summer? And it calls its name, Eternity.

Back when I was writing sermons every week I would take a break from my desk now and then and walk in the church's Memorial Garden. It provided a helpful retreat when plagued by writer's block, setting all kinds of things back into perspective. I still recall one particular Friday afternoon. Baseball practice was getting under way over on the adjoining college fields. In the playground, just beyond the yew hedge, excited nursery school children were clearing things away for the weekend. The distant bell in the college tower chimed the hour's passing. Busy insects buzzed their lazy farewell to yet another summer. I remember that I stood and scanned the names and dates listed upon that rough encircling wall, names that represented so much of my own life and ministry over the past years. I recalled somber moments when I recited "dust to dust" over those final resting places. I traced again those words carved on the central bronze plaque, "I am the resurrection and the life." I became profoundly aware of the river that runs through us all, that unrelenting river we call *Time*. "Who are you, and where are you going?" I asked myself.

The bells, the bees, the baseball bats, the restful beauty of that hallowed spot all answered me in their own way.

> You are a mixture, as were all of these whose final fragments you have laid to rest here, a compound of both nothingness and nobility, of foolishness and the finest possibilities of life. You are a part of all that is around you, the rugged wall, the trees and shrubs, the soil, the sunlight. Yet you are also more than that; you are the living mystery who asks these questions, attempts these answers. You are the one who senses in this early autumn sunlight, in this stillness and solemn beauty, something of eternity, a hope, and more than hope, a recognition that this instant set apart is of the essence of all moments, and that the One who is the resurrection and the life, who sweated great drops of blood within another garden for your sake, awaits you now, within this blessed moment, to greet you and to hold you in his everlasting arms.

Such moments come and go, they fade away. The choice we have is whether to believe them; to try to carry out into the turbulent river of the rest of days the message that they bear, or to dismiss them as the empty fantasies of a fall afternoon and go back to mere survival.

A river does run through us, its rapids, quiet pools and shallow places. As we launch out upon another year, twelve new months of wrestling with the demands and opportunities of calendar and clock, we need to recognize and claim such eternal moments for our own, to let them, more and more, shape and define whatever happens during the remainder of our days, brief or prolonged as they may be. So let us learn to live within God's promise as we inaugurate this new year of grace. Let us live our days as they are given to us, day, by day, by day, with joy, with trust, and with vision for the future, God's eternal future. So may we find blessing and a sign of hope, not only for ourselves, but for everyone whose life is touched by ours as we pass by.

∽

Guide us, O God, through every day of this new year so that, at its close, we may be nearer to your glory, and surer of our hope, our hope which is in Jesus Christ, our risen Lord and Savior. Amen.

Newsletter

January 1

Beginning again
is what it's all about,
picking up the scattered pieces
from where we let them fall,
joining jagged day to day
in hopes of calling them a year,
a living, even a life, more or less.

It doesn't do to remember too much.
Times like these can't last,
and cherishing only complicates
the daily things.

Select, perhaps, a glimpse,
a surprise, an open moment.
Save them for that point along
the way when they might just save you.
In the mean time, have a happy,
and we'll hope to see you again
next time around.

SHINING

This orb that drew us far across the ancient dark,
whose radiance was, at times, a comfort,
other times—it seemed—a mocking challenge,
endless burden, lure that led us on
toward despair, destruction, dreary death;
this celestial beam of light that came to rest—
no other way to put it—
where the golden god-child lay,
has never since departed.
Its burning,
after flaming forth at last about the feed box,
has now moved within,
kindled a blaze deep in these creaking bones
will not burn out until all darkness kneels and wonders.

ESSENCE

Yes, but what does it all boil down to in the end?
Five candles lit against the dark.
Christmas ribbons, colored paper
strewn across the hearth rug. An hour or so
with friends you have not seen since when,
and then, in all the crush, can catch only a word
before it's time to make tracks for the car.
A pile of pretty cards sharing
all too similar sentiments. Some tears
and turkey, holly, logs that burn (perhaps),
little faces lighted for an instant and,
through all of this, a word that murmurs,
"Wait" and "Hope" and "Keep a good look out."
Because of this, and taken all in all,
we couldn't, wouldn't want to,
live without it.

Bibliography

Barke, James, ed. *Poems and Songs of Robert Burns.* London and Glasgow: Collins, 1955.

Bauby, Jean-Dominique. *The Diving Bell and the Butterfly.* Translated by Jeremy Leggatt. New York: Knopf, 1997.

Boulding, Maria. *The Coming of God.* Conception, MO: Conception Abbey, 2000.

Dickens, Charles. *A Christmas Carol.* London: Chapman & Hall, 1843.

Frankl, Viktor. *Man's Search for Meaning. An Introduction to Logotherapy.* Boston: Beacon, 2006.

Giocondo, Giovanni. *A Letter to the Most Illustrious the Contessina Allagia degli Aldobrandeschi.* 1513. http://www.bartleby.com/73/1467.html.

Hayward, John, ed. *The Penguin Book of English Verse.* Harmondsworth, UK: Penguin, 1956.

Heschel, Abraham. *The Insecurity of Freedom: Essays on Human Existence.* New York: Farrar, Strauss & Giroux, 1959.

Johnson, Samuel. "No. 58: Expectation of Pleasure Frustrated." *The Idler,* May 26, 1759.

Khayyam, Omar. *Rubaiyat of Omar Khayyam.* Translated by Edward Fitzgerald. London: Collins, 1969.

Marquis. Don. *The Lives and Times of Archy and Mehitabel.* New York: Random House, 1940.

Nietzsche, Friedrich. *Twilight of the Idols.* Translated by Walter Kaufmann and R. J. Hollingdale. Turin, 1888. http://www.inp.uw.edu.pl/mdsie/Political_Thought/twilight-of-the-idols-friedrich-neitzsche.pdf.

Norris, Kathleen. *The Cloister Walk.* New York: Riverhead, 1996.

Steves, Rick. "Travel Writer Rick Steves Warns that Corporate Profiteering Comes with a Price." *Seattle Times,* January 3, 2015. http://www.seattletimes.com/opinion/guest-travel-writer-rick-steves-warns-that-corporate-profiteering-comes-with-a-price/.

Stone, Jon. *The Monster at the End of this Book.* Illustrated by Michael Smollin. New York: Random House, 1971.

Weschler, Lawrence. "Vermeer, the Light of Reason." *New York Times,* December 22, 1995.